THE MAN
FROM
INDIAN VALLEY

The Legend of Lester Rougeot

Michele L. Oksen

ISBN-10: 1477608176
ISBN-13: 978-1477608173

DEDICATION

The Man from Indian Valley, The Legend of Lester Rougeot
is dedicated to
Barbara Hatch Rougeot,
Regina Rougeot Bonds,
Chester Rougeot,
and Margie Rougeot LeRoux

CONTENTS

ACKNOWLEDGMENTS

Lester Rougeot would like to acknowledge the following people
for enriching his life with their friendship,
as well as their service and support of common causes:
Dick Avery, Walter Kauhn, Mike and the guys from the Paso Robles water
department, Paso Robles Lyons Club, Charlie Schmidt, Clarence Schmidt,
Tony Macera, Jules Delwiche, Francis McKanna, Jim Schmidt, John Wolf,
John Craspay, Robert Heeley, Ed Hale, Ole Viborg Construction Inc., Paul
Viborg Construction, Gene Gorbett, Raymond 'Skip' Dodd, Keith and Jaci
Rhyne, Brian Brown, Farm Supply, Mr. and Mrs. Frazier McGillvery,
John and Blanche Camino, Roho Construction, The Gomer Family,
Mitzi Page, Nicole Pazdan, Bruce Cinque, and Sue Cinque.

Thanks and acknowledgement are also due to the following people who
helped in the making and/or promotion of this book:
Melissa Chavez, Paso Robles Magazine and staff, Margie Rougeot,
Judy Miller, Emily Freeman, Dusty Rossi, Ken Freeman,
Alberta Bonnifield, Rohana Mayer, Dick Mason,
Kevin Will at KPRL and staff, Paso Robles Press and staff,
Jane Holton, Paula Cizmar, Patricia Heineman, Ken Renshaw,
the Rough Writers, Eric Oksen, Lloyd Oksen, and Gayle Oksen.

SPECIAL THANKS to Chester Rougeot
for his safe, sane, and most pleasurable chauffeur and tour guide skills.

EXTRA SPECIAL THANKS to Regina Rougeot Bonds
for her contributions to The Man from Indian Valley,
as well as her role as fact checker, editor, and chief cheerleader.

To Lester Ralph Rougeot,
For all the fine meals at Joe's Places, for the Grange Hall pancake
breakfasts, for your leap of faith, for your trust, and for your encouragement
– I give you heartfelt thanks.
It was truly a pleasure, and an honor, to pen your story.
Your friend,
Michele Oksen

1 – GRANDDAD'S GUIDANCE

"My grandfather was the person who inspired me most in my life. I had an admiration for what he accomplished. He had a purpose in life." The man from Indian Valley, the most recognizable community character around Paso Robles, looked up, humbled by memories of his maternal grandfather. He sat with his hands on the table next to his mother's tattered black and white photo album, the brim of his straw cowboy hat an awning over his sincere blue eyes. "Grandpa was a self-made man. He never did graduate from school, you know, never went past the third grade, but he ended up owning four ranches around here. He was very energetic and confident about whatever he was doin'," he said. "Grandpa helped a lot of people."

At first glance, Lester Ralph Rougeot could be perceived as just another good ol' boy, complete with pointy boots and suspenders, and up until October of 2011 fat cigars. Upon further investigation, his deep-seated code of conduct was revealed as he recited stories from his past. Somehow, and he was amazed by this, people expressed interest in his life and his observations and outlooks. They encouraged him to tell his tale.

Lester's face brightened as he spoke of Rega Dent Freeman. Though nearly seven decades had passed since he lived with his grandfather, during his 1942/1943 senior year at Paso Robles High School, Lester recalled their relationship as one of mutual appreciation and respect.

"Grandpa said I was the only one who ever started and finished a job," Lester remembered. "He depended on me to get things done." Rega was impressed with his grandson and the feeling was shared. Lester considered his grandfather a standard of manhood from which to assess his own progress.

LESTER RALPH ROUGEOT 2005

"Grandpa was a man who said somethin' and that was it," Lester said. He pointed his finger at a black and white photograph of his grandfather. "He had a lot of wisdom about what he was doin'. Everybody looked up to him. I learned to be fair with everybody and be honest about everything. Grandpa taught me a lot about that."

REGA DENT FREEMAN

It was Granddad's guidance, not livestock or land, that Rega bestowed on Lester. The gift of a priceless set of principles and values is what Lester would live by throughout his life. In addition, Rega had provided Lester with moral support, praise, trust, and a bond that served to empower and embolden Lester, during his formative years.

Lester's grandfather helped shape his apprentice grandson, by example. When Rega took charge of situations, or took action for or against something, or took it upon himself to promote and fund projects, Lester paid attention.

"My grandparents started the first Grange Halls in the area," Lester said with pride in his smile. "They donated a lot of time and they contacted the State Grange for funding of the Estrella Grange. And it was my grandmother who loaned money to buy the Grange in Paso."

It was official. Northern San Luis Obispo County then had meeting places where local farmers could congregate, keep informed, and participate in productive causes. Though Lester, himself, was just a rambunctious boy at the time, a child who might have preferred to get into mischief, he was influenced by this important community development.

Grange activities intrigued young Lester. He aspired to join as soon as he was of age. Which he did. Decades later, he is still dedicated to Grange goals. Lester's sense of stewardship and protectiveness of the El Paso de Robles Grange Hall, in particular, went public in 1990. It was after the last dance at the Paso Robles Hall, which as it turned out, was the last Grange dance in all of San Luis Obispo County.

"I told 'em 'I'll shut the place down if you have another dance'," Lester said. At that time, he was State Deputy to the Master of the California State Grange, with the authority to make good on his promise to lock the doors. "Dues and dances had been makin' money for the Grange, but people got out of hand, destructive. Chairs were broken and the cops were called."

The dances had lost the feeling of community, the camaraderie they once intended. So, perhaps like his grandfather might have done, Lester put his foot down. He would not allow disrespect or destruction of the El Paso de Robles Grange Hall. Oh no, not on his watch. Practicality played a part in his decision – as did sentimentality. Consequently, tradition changed. Just like that.

In lieu of dances, that had been gainful fundraisers for the Grange, Lester came up with the idea of a monthly pancake breakfast. The plan was approved and implemented. Members of the various local 4-H clubs were enlisted to serve the food and beverages, which not only helped the Grange earn funds, it was a way for 4-Hers to earn points toward advancement within their organization. Soon, every second Sunday of every month, there was a calm, friendly gathering of supporters who met at the Grange, where they enjoyed stacks of pancakes, bacon, eggs, orange juice, and coffee.

Twenty-two years later – the tradition lives on.

"Besides starting the first Grange Halls in the area, my grandparents, Rega and Dovie, they're the ones who got money to start San Luis Obispo County's first fair," Lester noted. Now, it's Lester who is supports the fair in several ways. One of which is as a volunteer facilitator of a fair sponsored free pancake breakfast in the park, manned by Grange volunteers. No small task as the turnout has been upward of sixteen hundred breakfasts, served on a single three hour morning. The event is intended to promote business to downtown merchants, as locals and out-of-towners flock to the Mid State Fair. As of 2012, Lester will have volunteered his pancake breakfast expertise to the fair for nineteen years.

When Rega Freeman sponsored and mentored his grandson through the years in Future Farmers of America, Rega took pride in Lester's successes; the blue ribbons, the awards, the recognitions of excellence, and the State Farmer's Degree, to name a few. "He was in my corner one hundred percent," Lester said. Consequently, Lester's skill level and knowledge rose tremendously in his grandfather's company. Rega had faith in his grandson's intellect and ingenuity. He trusted Lester's common sense. That trust, encouraged Lester to explore possibilities, rather than accept limitations. This built on Lester's self-confidence, something Lester would later do for his own children and the children in his community.

So appreciative of his grandfather, Lester again followed in Rega's footsteps when he became actively involved in support of agriculturally oriented youth activities. Not only did Lester help raise funds by coordinating barbeques and breakfasts, as well as auctioneering cookies, he and his wife, Barbara, were instrumental in the building of a park and a campground for use by children.

Husband and wife, Lester and Barbara, also supported children by buying pigs, prospective fair animals, that hadn't made the weight required to compete. They even bought animals they didn't intend to eat.

"Even on her death bed, Auntie Barbara could hardly wait to get to the fair, to the auction, so they could buy an animal then give it back to the kid," Judy Miller said. "She could hardly make it but it didn't matter."

"My great niece, Meagan Miller, had a replacement heifer she'd raised from a calf," Lester began. "We paid three thousand dollars for that heifer." The Rougeot's didn't need a replacement heifer; they were not in the cattle business. They couldn't bring themselves to butcher, package, and freeze the valuable bovine either. Instead they gave the animal back to Meagan with the agreement that the money would go toward college. "Meagan raised several calves out of that heifer. She named her first bull calf 'Lester' and I told her she better never castrate him." Lester laughed.

Lester and Barbara also took part in The Ranchita 4-H's annual cookie auction where Barbara liked to buy baked goods, at prices that made the auctioneer's eyes pop. Lester, the auctioneer, was the one who egged on cookie lovers, entertained himself, encouraging husbands and wives to, unknowingly, bid against each other until he banged the gavel down and said, "Sold to the highest bidder." When the highest bidder was his own wife, Barbara, the couple would then turn right around and re-donate the high dollar sweets to someone they knew would enjoy them.

"The Ranchita cookie auction used to make about four hundred dollars," Lester stated. "Now they make four thousand to five thousand. The money goes to fund the kids for their fair projects."

Instead of splurging on new gadgets, glamorous clothes, or luxurious material objects for their pleasure, Lester and Barbara derived joy from supporting causes. It wasn't unusual for the couple to do it on the sly either, and swear others to secrecy. But, as luck would have it - someone squealed and divulged the Rougeots were most generous with their donations. In fact, one year Barbara was so determined to outbid the competition, the Rougeot's ended up paying hundreds of dollars for a single cake embellished with a creative and edible farm scene on top.

"Uncle Lester and Auntie Barbara went to every cookie auction," Judy stated. "He auctioneered and she bought stuff. To make money for the 4-H, she bid on this huge white sheet cake with coconut frosting, a pig, and a horse, and a sheep out of peanut butter cookies and a little bridge like a trail class, all sorts of neat stuff. A friend of ours made it so it was really good. She's a baker. Uncle Lester paid four hundred dollars for this damn cake and brought it to where I worked." Judy shook her head and beamed. "They were always helpin' the kids."

"You know, when my granddad was a kid, he grew up in Texas," Lester disclosed and pointed his finger at a page in his mother's photo album. The old and fibrous black paper page had the corners of several black and white images, of Lester's grandparents, tucked into tiny glued-on triangular pockets.

"Rega Dent Freeman was born December 24, 1874, in Indian Springs, Butts County, Georgia," Regina Rougeot Bonds reported. "From Georgia the family moved to Graham, Young County, Texas, where they bought three thousand acres to farm and raise livestock. While in Texas, Dad's great grandparents, Thomas and Sarah Freeman, prospered. Their brand was SOS which was later changed to S on the hip and shoulder. The children, including Rega, were reared on the stock ranch where they learned to ride the range and care for the cattle, as well as attend public school."

Of course, that's not all they were exposed to. Reading, writing, and arithmetic were part of the children's educational program but so was life, at a time in Texas, when lawlessness ran unbridled.

"While in Texas, Great Great Grandpa Thomas Freeman also served as President of the 'Vigilantes'," Regina revealed, "an organization that co-operated with various elected authorities and waged relentless war on bandits until they were driven out of the state."

When necessary, citizens, such as Thomas, discouraged train robbers, horse thieves, murderers, and cattle rustlers any way they could, even by way of shoot outs and hanging trees.

Thomas' son, Rega, Lester's grandfather, the man he looked up to and emulated, had not only been raised to work hard and prosper, he had grown up a witness to frontier justice. As a child, Rega, learned that a swift method of judging guilt or innocence, often followed by immediate punishment for wrong doings, was reasonable and just; it deterred misbehavior. And yet, as Lester was quick to recount, his grandfather's temperament was neither hostile nor harsh, but rather he was tolerant, approachable, and fair.

"Grandpa Freeman had a good sense of humor." Lester remembered. "He was fun to be around. He was always pullin' stuff."

"It was on November 18, 1878, that Rega Dent Freeman married Malissa Dovie Nicklas. Malissa Dovie, who went by Dovie, was born and raised in Palo Pinto County, Texas," Regina detailed. "They stayed there until 1902, when they sold out and began the process of moving west."

First, Rega and his brother, Joe Freeman, had moved to California, where they leased the H. A. Fallon Ranch in Bradley, leaving Rega's young wife, and second daughter, in Texas. The couple's first daughter, Bonnie, had died in childbirth. When Rega returned to Texas to get Dovie, and their daughter, Ona, Dovie became pregnant with another daughter, Thelma. The family secretly stowed themselves in a train's box car and rode with the hay for the mules. They had to be very quiet so they would not have to pay train fare.

REGA DENT FREEMAN
MALISSA DOVIE NICKLAS FREEMAN
NOVEMBER 18, 1878

As the story goes, they stopped in Arizona, with their mules, to farm south of Roosevelt Lake, as well as haul cement and supplies for the Roosevelt Dam, which was in the beginning phase of construction. In Arizona the Freemans stayed until they had enough money to proceed to the land Rega had leased in Bradley, California. While near Globe, Arizona, they lived in a tent where their daughter, Thelma, was born December 9, 1903.

Thelma later told her granddaughter, Regina, a story about a shepherd dog that was in Arizona when they lived in the tent. "My mother said the dog didn't like Indians and slept in the tent with us," Thelma told Regina. "One night he heard an old Indian man snoring. My mother crawled over to get a knife out of the trunk. The trunk lid made a noise and the dog made two yelps and was gone."

After Arizona, the young Freeman family and their mules boarded another train. This time bound for California. Again, they were stowaways, who had to remain quiet for the duration of the trip, which was likely even more challenging with baby Thelma aboard.

"Once the family made their way back to Bradley, Thelma's father, Rega and his brother, Joe Freeman purchased the ranch they had leased. It was right about the time of the 1906 earthquake," Regina stated. "Shortly thereafter, Rega bought out his brother's interest in the land and began to acquire more property piece by piece. Rega and Dovie Freeman's family grew over the years to include Ona, Thelma, Richard, Eugene, Ralph, Ernest and Rega D. "Babe" Freeman.

"At the age of thirteen, my mother's younger brother, Ralph, was killed in a car accident several miles from San Miguel, in Lowes Canyon," Lester said. "The car tipped over and his neck was broken."

By autumn of 1910, Rega had moved his family to their Pleasant Valley Ranch where his children could walk to the Pleasant Valley and Ranchita Schools.

Just four years after Rega and Dovie had settled into their Pleasant Valley Ranch, in January of 1914, the territory endured severe flooding. The torrential rain caused widespread property damage and interrupted telephone service. Not only small country road bridges over tributaries, creeks, and gorges, but railroad trestles and major bridges that spanned the Salinas River, including the bridges at San Ardo and Bradley, had washed away. The course of the river changed as raging water and debris slammed into the banks taking valuable farm land along with it.

Though rural citizens were cut off from communications and roads were closed in nearly every direction, the hearty country folks in the area managed to survive. Perhaps they even bonded as they helped each other rebuild, repair, and recover from the natural disaster.

SAN MIGUEL BRIDGE 1914

"The Lowes put on grain sacks for swimmin' suits and went across the river hangin' on to a rope to get everybody's mail," Lester recounted. Neighborly people up and down the Salinas River had constructed cable systems over which they sent food and supplies to the other side.

At the time, Thomas and Ida May Rougeot, Lester's paternal grandparents, lived at their twenty-six hundred acre ranch on Ranchita Canyon Road up Hog Canyon in Monterey County, where their children attended nearby schools.

According to Lester's daughter, Regina's research, the seventh child of Cadet and Sarah Rougeot, Lester's grandfather, "Thomas Henry Rougeot was said to have had the advantage of Glenmore, New York's public schools until he was eighteen years old. Thereafter, he decided to head west and set out for Colorado in 1882, where he stayed with his brother John for six years. There Thomas spent much of that time lumbering in Jefferson County. In 1888, Thomas journeyed west to join his brothers, Theodore and John, who had moved to Estrella, San Luis Obispo County, California ahead of him.

Thomas and John rented land in the Estrella area and began to farm. In 1891, when Thomas was twenty-seven years old he married a twenty-three year old woman named Ida May Shuey at her family's ranch in Monterey County, California.

THOMAS ROUGEOT AND IDA MAY SHUEY 1891

"Ida May's parents, Josephus and Sarah Newland Shuey, had come across the plains from Illinois in a covered wagon pulled by an ox team in 1859. They first settled in Contra Costa County, California, but by 1885, they had relocated to Echo Canyon."

Where's Echo Canyon?

"Echo Canyon," Lester revealed, "is now known as Hog Canyon."

"Thomas gradually obtained a footing and a good farming outfit until 1895 when he leased land at the head of Keyes Canyon, San Luis Obispo County, California," Regina said. "He farmed there until 1901 when he then purchased his first one hundred sixty acres in nearby Echo Canyon."

The land, according to Lester, was approximately three miles to the south of Thomas' in-law's, the Shuey's ranch.

"Thomas and his wife, Ida May, had eight children - Sarah, Donald, Frank, Ada, Clarence Theodore – born November 2, 1901 in Hog Canyon, Monterey County, California, twins Fay and Ray, and Wilma.

"Over the years, an enterprising and successful Thomas purchased adjoining land until his holdings totaled two thousand six hundred acres of southern Monterey County where he built a residence and barns for his livestock as well as hay and grain storage."

"Grandpa Rougeot raised Shorthorn Durham cattle," Lester said. It was a breed that, at the time, was suitable for both beef and dairy. "He also had a well-bred Jack from Kentucky for breeding purposes and became well known for his mules."

While in the Echo Canyon/Hog Canyon area Thomas, along with H.H. Russell, proposed a county road project to supervisors which was accepted and established. Later, Thomas promoted a Star Route mail service, as well as the Interurban Telephone Company for which he was the president for four years.

A believer in the benefits of education, Thomas was a trustee for the Ellis School District, until he sold his land to John Work. Thomas thought it would be best if he moved his family to San Luis Obispo, so his children could pursue higher education at California Polytechnic School. In 1920 Thomas' son, Clarence (Lester's father), went to California Polytechnic School to further his education and play college baseball. Clarence's brother and sister, Ray and Fay (the twins), also went to Cal Poly.

Lester flipped the page on the old photo album and leaned forward. "This one is my grandparent's house in San Luis Obispo," he said and pointed. "It's on Santa Rosa, that's Bishop Peak in the background." Lester leaned back in his chair, pushed his hat back and revealed his blue eyes and a bit of forehead. "One year, Grandpa Rougeot borrowed a team of horses, a wagon, plow, and harrow from a friend of his and had me drive it across San Luis Obispo, Broad Street, to his house to work the garden to the South of the house. He liked to grow corn, tomatoes, and cucumbers, all sorts of stuff he grew. There was a family orchard in back, too. Lemons, pears, peaches, apricots..." Lester shook his head and smiled. With a sudden and distinct warm and affectionate tone he added, "Grandma, she was a doll. She was always makin' buttermilk cookies." According to Lester, his grandmother, Ida May Shuey Rougeot, managed the house and was always there and available.

THOMAS AND IDA MAY ROUGEOT'S HOUSE
SAN LUIS OBISPO – BISHOP PEAK IN BACKGROUND

Thomas died May 3, 1948 in San Luis Obispo, California, where his wife, Ida May, also died three years later, March 1, 1951.

Though their son, Clarence, had moved with them from the Echo Canyon/Hog Canyon area to San Luis Obispo, Clarence always considered home to be the area where he was born and where he had spent his childhood. When the opportunity to return presented itself, Clarence seized it. He quit school to go to work for his brother-in-law, Otto Dauth, an Estrella farmer and stockman. Clarence then moved back up to the northern most reaches of San Luis Obispo County where his heartstrings were still attached and his roots had been firmly planted.

Shortly after Clarence began work for the Dauths, during

1922's summer grain harvest, his sister, Sarah Rougeot Dauth died. Her absence meant a neighboring rancher's daughter, Sarah Thelma Freeman, was called on to cook for the work crew. Thelma was a young woman whom Clarence had gone to school with as a child. They became reacquainted during harvest season.

"The first time I saw Clarence was when we were in grade school at the Ellis School," Lester's mother, Thelma, told her granddaughter, Regina. "He was a little boy with knee pants on."

ELLIS SCHOOL STUDENTS - APPROXIMATELY 1909
SECOND ROW FROM TOP - ELSIE VON DOLLEN, BELLA ELLIS, GRACE STEWART, ALICE WORK. THIRD ROW FROM TOP – EMMA VON DOLLEN, CLARENCE ROUGEOT, BERNICE STEWART, LAWRENCE HUSTON, ADA ROUGEOT. BOTTOM ROW – HOPE STEWART, RAY ROUGEOT, FAY ROUGEOT

No longer awkward and knobby kneed children, Clarence and Thelma attended to their jobs at the Dauth Ranch, where they became attracted to each other. Both looked forward to meals when they could sneak peeks at one another and have occasions to flash smiles in each other's direction. Before long they became engaged to be married.

CLARENCE ROUGEOT AT THE PARKFIELD RODEO - 1922
CARS USED AS A FENCE IN BACKGROUND

PARKFIELD RODEO – 1922

Announcement of their impending nuptials did not set well with Thelma's father, Rega Freeman. Whether it was simply a matter of no one being good enough for his daughter, or an issue with something he felt was objectionable about her betrothed, remains a mystery. However, without doubt Rega realized a marriage between

15

Thelma and Clarence Rougeot, meant his competent daughter would no longer be his helper, but would become Clarence's helpmate. The thought of losing his daughter made Rega so unhappy, he decided to put both Thelma and her older sister, Ona, on a train bound for Texas.

SISTERS - ONA AND THELMA FREEMAN

In hopes a couple months of separation would clear his daughter's heart and mind of the man Rega felt was an inappropriate match for Thelma, the two sisters were sent to visit family that September, first to Texas and then Colorado, to see Uncle Jewel Nicklas, Thelma's mother's brother.

THELMA AND ONA'S TRIP – COLORADO OCTOBER 1922

When the sisters returned to Paso Robles, they got off the train. At one end of the station, they saw their father, Rega, standing in wait of their arrival. Though Thelma respected her father and would have done most anything to keep from disappointing him, her heart was aflutter when she looked in the other direction, and there was Clarence Rougeot standing his ground, as well.

Absence had not made Thelma's heart go yonder as her father had intended. Rather the separation had done quite the opposite. It had, indeed, made her heart grow fonder. The exhilaration Thelma felt when she saw the man she loved waiting to give her a ride home, was something even her father could see. Right then and there Rega knew his plan had failed. His strong-willed and passionate daughter disobeyed his wishes and went with Clarence.

For the next few weeks, while still employed by his brother-in-law Otto, Clarence courted Thelma. Otto, being a recent widower, had decided to leave the farming business behind and shortly thereafter opened the Paso Robles Laundry. He sold his farming equipment to Clarence who became a self-employed farmer. After which, on November 2, 1922, Clarence and Thelma obtained a marriage license and three days later, on November 5, 1922 they were married.

THOMAS FREEMAN, CLARENCE ROUGEOT,
THELMA FREEMAN ROUGEOT, FAY ROUGEOT,
AND REVEREND GOODELL BEHIND

At Thelma's parent's ranch, the Freeman Ranch, located in Pleasant Valley near Estrella, Reverend. E.D. Goodell, a Methodist Minister of the Estrella Church, officiated the ceremony. As told by Thelma to her granddaughter, Regina, "Margaret, my younger sister, couldn't understand why I got a ring out of my box and she didn't."

Following Clarence and Thelma's wedding, the family, including Rega who had come to, at best half-heartedly, accept the marriage, enjoyed an outdoor dinner along the north side of the house at tables set with place cards and decorative baskets of nuts and candy.

CLARENCE ROUGEOT DRIVING MULES – 1924

CLARENCE ROUGEOT CAUSING EXCITEMENT

The happy couple moved into what was known as the Rice Place in Indian Valley. There they rented from Mr. Tutin until they lost the lease because of a barley deal - something about Rega, Thelma's father, and a discrepancy over seed.

Right about that same time, in 1924, when Thelma's older sister announced her plans to marry, their father, Rega voiced his objections, yet again, and refused to attend his daughter, Ona's wedding.

After leaving Indian Valley, Clarence, Thelma, and their baby, Gladys, moved into a house in Lowe's Canyon, an isolated location where the terrain was suitable for dry farming grain. There, just two canyons to the west, approximately ten miles as the crow flies, of Clarence's birth place, in a small ranch house made of solid and thick wood boards is where Lester Ralph Rougeot's story begins.

2 – THE WATERMELON WAGER

Tests of tolerance and tenacity were as plentiful as flies on manure. Only those who had some sand chose the lifestyle – and survived. Hot days spent in full sun, unforeseen yet inevitable equipment malfunctions, dust in every crack, dried out skin, calloused hands, it didn't matter if you were a man, woman, or child, when you lived on the Clarence Rougeot farm, you toiled. And toil it was to assure a harvest of as much wheat and barley as their fields would yield.

GRAIN HARVEST

It was July of 1925, and the land at Lowe's Canyon, Monterey County, California , just north of the San Luis Obispo County line was farmable but was far from level or free from rock. Clarence drove a team of up to thirty-six mules to pull the harvester around those hills. Days were long and nights were short on the farm, especially that time of year.

Clarence's wife, Thelma, who worked as hard as her husband, did everything she possibly could during that harvest. Though not her usual nimble self, she wasn't on the couch eating bon bons or out being pampered or primped. Sure some tender loving care would have been nice, but that's not the way it was. Thelma, an equal partner in every sense of the meaning, toughed out the heat and the hustle, alongside her man, until she was forced, by nature, to attend to another task.

During those early years of farming Lowe's Canyon, it was Calvin Coolidge who was the country's thirtieth president. He had been the first in the United States of America to have his inauguration broadcast on radio. Televisions were not yet a common domestic device and movies of the day, such as the Western *The Lucky Horseshoe* starring Tom Mix and the comedy *The Gold Rush* starring Charlie Chaplin, were played in theatres as silent films. Appropriately for the Rougeot's a popular song, originally written in 1925, was titled *Yes, Sir, That's My Baby.*

CLARENCE AND THELMA ROUGEOT

For Clarence, also known as Stub because of his short stature, that harvest season was an exciting time. Thelma was nearing the due date of their second child. Though the couple was filled with pride over Gladys Fay, their adored blonde haired, blue eyed daughter, it wasn't a secret they hoped their next child would be a son. The pregnancy as well as Thelma's expanded waist line gave the harvest crew something to tease Clarence about. Fully aware of his desire to have a son the hired help entertained each other by taunts that the baby would surely be another girl.

Soon Clarence and the crew began to volley good natured bets. Certain that Thelma was going to birth a boy, Clarence took the crew up on their wager. If the child was a girl he would go nine miles to the nearest town of San Miguel and buy a watermelon. If the child was a boy the crew was to make the trip and the purchase.

On July 20, 1925, inside thick and solid timber walls of their Lowe's Canyon house, Thelma went into labor. She delivered their second child, a blonde haired blue eyed baby. Not such a surprise perhaps. That is until she continued to birth yet another child with dark hair and blue eyes.

CHESTER AND LESTER ROUGEOT

Twins! And much to the couples delight, they were both boys. First Chester Clarence Rougeot, and then Lester Ralph Rougeot came into the world, Chester with blonde hair, Lester with darker hair.

* * *

22

"This is the house I was born in," Lester said as he stepped down from the passenger seat of his son's pickup. He marveled at the old house. It was the first stop on a tour of the area where Lester was raised. Lester's son, Chester, was the designated driver, Lester the tour guide. "That was over eighty-six years ago. The place held up good."

Lester's own solid frame has endured the test of time as well. He sauntered toward his birth house, over to the front porch where he peered inside the glassless window frame inside a room littered with broken boards, box springs, and an old ragged and stained mattress. Long since abandoned by humans, the structure houses a resident barn owl that swooped down from the rafters out a hole between two boards in one of the walls.

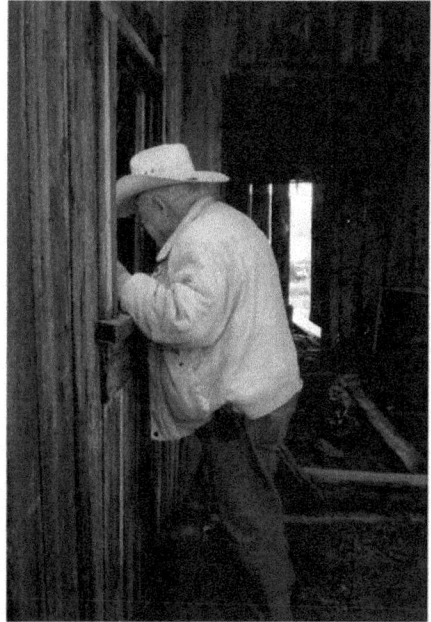

LESTER ROUGEOT EXPLORES HIS 1925 BIRTH HOUSE
IN LOWES CANYON – 2012

Outside the house, in the yard, looking north up Lowes Canyon, the terrain, like a groove in the earth that drew the eye toward the distant Cholame Hills, persuaded a sense of serenity.

Surrounding the house were the grassy fields that on Lester's 1925 day of birth, were covered in tall stalks of grain in the process of being harvested. Inflated with pride, Clarence went to those fields and made the announcement.

"Boys! Two of them," he shouted. Cheers ensued as backs were slapped and ribs were elbowed. Clarence brothers-in-law insisted the harvest crew pay up with not only one watermelon, but two. Which, with joy, they did and the celebration began.

THELMA ROUGEOT WITH CHESTER AND LESTER ROUGEOT

After Lowe's Canyon, the Clarence Rougeot family moved southeast a few miles into San Luis Obispo County to the Foley place in Hog Canyon. There Clarence and Thelma continued to farm grain as their family grew from five to six, when baby Mildred joined the family. Two daughters and two sons blessed the couple around the house and the farm.

ONA FREEMAN WITH CHESTER ROUGEOT
THELMA FREEMAN ROUGEOT WITH LESTER ROUGEOT

LESTER AND CHESTER ROUGEOT

LOWES CANYON SQUIRREL HUNTERS
CHESTER, GLADYS, AND LESTER ROUGEOT – 1927

Although fraternal not identical, the twin boys were often dressed in matching jumpsuits or coveralls. Lester with a head full of brown hair and Chester with blonde, the twins doubled the family's happiness - and the challenges.

As expected for inquisitive boys who had access to the great outdoors, and working parents, there were a multitude of opportunities for activities that started out like fun.

GLADYS, CHESTER, LESTER, AND MILDRED ROUGEOT

"It was in the late 1920's when we were three or four years old," Lester began. "My mother was off with my dad workin' the farm and a girl who lived nearby named Ruth Quenser had been hired to cook and care for us."

Lester mentioned Ruth's brother, Albert Quenser, also had occasion to help Clarence around the Rougeot's ranch.

Just a young girl of about thirteen years of age, Ruth had her hands full with the Rougeot children that day, especially the twin boys.

"I have no idea what Chester and I had gotten into, but it must have been pretty bad because Ruth got a switch after us and chased us out in the yard. We finally escaped by climbin' up a cypress tree."

Although he remembers a switch wielding Ruth run after them, the particulars of the twins' mischief wasn't what left an impression on Lester. What did stick with him was the fact that the boys' disobedience and refusal to climb back down that tree made Ruth even angrier.

CHESTER AND LESTER ROUGEOT

They sat high in the pruned tree, way out of Ruth's reach. It wasn't until their mother, Thelma, came home that the boys even considered coming back down. Perhaps it was the voice of authority that reasoned with them or maybe it was their increasing discomfort of being perched like bear cubs on branches. Whatever it was that convinced them Lester said, "When we were finally coaxed out of the tree it was to the wrath of Ruth and Momma."

RANCHITA SCHOOLHOUSE

For the first grade, twins, Lester and Chester, attended Ranchita School where Lester said, "My mother went there too when she was a girl." Sometime after Lester and his siblings went to Ranchita School it closed its doors to students and, "Sold to a guy who moved it and made a bunkhouse out of it."

The landscape, that in 2012, is covered in straight rows of grape vines was once lush shoots of grain in the spring or rich golden mature stalks in the summer. Far fewer houses, narrower roads, not as much evidence of man as there is today, those were some of the things that were different during Lester's childhood.

Gentle and open, the terrain of Hog Canyon and Von Dollen Roads was a patchwork of Clarence's Onis wheat and Hero barley fields among oak studded rolling hills. The wheat variety was a type that produced high grain yields and tolerated high temperatures, little rainfall, and no irrigation. "The barbless barley was grown for the horses," Lester mentioned.

GRAIN HARVESTER OPERATOR CLARENCE ROUGEOT

MULE TEAM PULLS HARVESTER

Although much of the suitable farm ground in the area had been planted in grain, by Clarence and neighboring farmers, it looked as if nature was responsible for the uncomplicated countryside. Hills were vivid green with grasses and grains that fluttered on the breeze in a fluid motion much like the ripples over deep water.

A peaceful place where deer grazed, crops grew, and neighbors were far and few between each other, Hog Canyon, Ranchita Canyon, and in between the two - the area also known as part of Pleasant Valley - was a great place for children to roam around and explore.

On one such exploration, in a canyon behind the house, Lester's twin brother, Chester, decided to take a stick and poke it in a hole of a felled old oak tree.

Immediately on the war path, angry honey bees shot out of their hive in hot pursuit of the offender. But the culprit, Lester told, "He had squatted down by the stump of the tree and they never bothered him." The bees buzzed right over the top of Chester.

Lester began to swat something around the side of his face as he recounted the sequence of events. "I took off runnin' like hell," he said.

Lester ran. Chester crouched. The bees had only one person available to chase - the one who fled.

The sound of the hive's defensive troops might as well have been as loud as big wide monster truck tires steadily speeding up a straight and newly smoothed and sealed asphalt road. Hummm...the drone of bees got louder and louder. *Run, Lester's instincts told him, run. Faster, faster.*

But there was no getting away. Bees dive bombed him even as he swatted furiously. And they stung him all right - right behind the ear. When Lester had distanced himself far enough away from the bee hive and the bees that had chased him, he looked back to see Chester tucked safely at the base of the tree.

"He was laughin' like crazy," Lester recalled with a grin as he rubbed his ear. "Man my ear swelled up."

Bee stings or not it was back to work when the twins got home.

"Everyone had chores or jobs on a working ranch," Lester stated. "When I was about four or five years old, I drove a buckeye seeder. I would drive the mules and Dad would walk behind kickin' the weeds out of the teeth."

Among the weeds, turkey mullein, a pungent, low growing, pale greenish gray weed would jam up the teeth of the ripper. Although turkey mullein seeds are a food source for wild birds and small mammals, the plant itself is undesirable in hay and grain fields. Livestock avoid it on abundant range ground but when fed hay contaminated with turkey mullein, it can cause problems in the digestive track.

At any rate, Clarence had to remove the tangle of weeds before he could plant grain seeds. He needed a driver and who better than his competent son, Lester? There was so much to be done on any given day, that his own hands were not enough, and over time Clarence grew dependant on Lester. His capable son was not only adept at farm work, he was willing and proud to be working alongside his father. Chester, on the other hand, was more interested in helping Thelma.

"We had a bird's eggs collection," Lester recalled. "One day when they were poisoning squirrels, old Hugo Lichti climbed up a big tree on the ranch where there was an eagle's nest. He got up there and stole an egg then pulled out his pistol and started shootin'. My dad was so mad."

Although it may have seemed so at times, life at the Rougeot's wasn't all work and no play. As Lester remembered the assortment of eggs he and Chester had gathered over the years he revealed, "We had everything. A quail's egg, dove, bluebird, blue jay, and that eagle egg. All those eggs we had." It was with pride that the boys displayed the collection in their room.

Ever the farmer's sons, Lester and Chester, liked to amuse themselves in the sand at the creek with their homemade toy farm equipment. Unlike today's children, no plastic toys littered their living room or yard.

Instead, it was sticks or pieces of scrap lumber that were fastened together, some with a nail driven through that would serve as a ripper, some with oblong pieces that were the tracks on tractors. The twins' toy plows and tractors were used to make furrows in the dirt, on a smaller scale but, much like the ones their father's made in the fields.

THE ROUGEOT CHILDREN

Among the menagerie of animals in the Rougeot's farmyard, Chick the saddle horse was worth bragging rights in the family.

"Chick was the first horse my dad had after he was married," Lester said.

CHICK THE SADDLE HORSE WITH THE ROUGEOT CHILDREN

Gentle enough to pack around four children, yet tough enough to handle the demands on a working ranch horse, Chick was a trusty steed. Clarence roped cattle off Chick. After he dallied his rope and dismounted, he knew he could depend on the stout horse to keep the rope taut, thus the bovine still, for purposes of doctoring, marking, branding, or castrating.

CHICK AT WORK

Along with the horses that were used for work around the ranch, there were cattle for beef, hogs for pork, and the family had ten to twelve milk cows. It was Lester and Chester's responsibility to milk those cows, morning and night. Thelma would then hop in the car and haul the cream to town to supplement their income.

THELMA ROUGEOT WITH HER FLOCK OF CHICKS

The Rougeot's do-it-yourself operation also included an orchard, a vegetable garden, and poultry for eggs and meat.

Though the feathered flock was mostly chickens, Lester recalled an old Tom turkey that lived on the ranch. That old Tom was mean. Every time Lester had to walk near him the turkey attacked. His spurs gouged, wings flapped, and beak struck at Lester who figured someday that old bird would draw blood.

Finally, Lester had enough. When the turkey came after him again he was ready to give the bird an attitude adjustment. Tom attacked and Lester took an old board and swung. Whack! Old Tom went flying across the yard and landed in the dirt with a thud. And there he stayed, silent, and still. It appeared old Tom was a goner. After looking over his shoulder and all around Lester was relieved to see he was alone. He leaned down and picked up a limp and lifeless Tom by the legs.

"I threw 'im in the crick," Lester said. He didn't plan to tell anyone what happened.

Two hours after the turkey's supposed demise, Lester went into the yard again. To his surprise, there was that old Tom pecking the ground as if nothing had happened. The only difference – he'd seen the light and decided to let Lester be.

"Good thing I didn't kill 'im," Lester said, "'cause I was scared."

Just boys gathering bird eggs, building toys out of whatever available materials they could find, and playing in the creekside sand and mud, yet, in Lester's and Chester's cases, they were also depended on to contribute around the ranch. Their sense of responsibility began early in life. No strangers to a long hard workday, their feet had to hit the floor at a run from a very young age. A typical day, during harvest, started well before dawn. By four in the morning the boys were out the door.

"We got up and headed to the barn to get the mules curried, fed, and harnessed up for the day's work," Lester recalled. "We would come back in after the chores and Momma would have a big breakfast waitin' for us. Red eyed gravy, steak, eggs, taters and biscuits. After a hearty meal, we would head to the fields to cut the grain or hay. At the end of the day the animals all had to be tended to before supper."

CLARENCE ROUGEOT FARMING WITH MULE TEAM

CLARENCE ROUGEOT

CLARENCE ROUGEOT HARVESTER OPERATOR

HOG CANYON HARVEST

Back in the late 1920's and early 1930's horsepower on the Rougeot Ranch meant actual hay eating manure makers. Top of the line mules were used to muscle around the various equipment. Unlike some irrigated and more level farms closer to the Salinas River, the many acres of the Rougeot grain fields were dry farmed on gentle slopes. The heavy wooden harvester had to be pulled by a team of up to thirty-six mules. That's when a day's work took grit. Everyone had to pitch in wherever and whenever they could and Lester was no exception.

"I figured I'd help the guys out a little at the end of the harvest day," Lester said.

After a long day of pulling a bulky wooden harvester in the hot sun, up and down hills of wheat or barley the mules were tired. Heavy harnesses rubbed the same sore spots day in and day out. Dried salty sweat made them itchy and added to their irritability and reputed stubbornness. And who wouldn't be hard to control and a touch on the cantankerous side after a day like that?

Well, Lester wanted to discourage any dragging hooves. The sooner the team got into the barn the quicker everyone could get some rest so they could do it all again the next day. He decided it'd be helpful to hurry the mules along.

Not that any working mule or horse ever needed to be encouraged or persuaded to rush back to the barn to their bucket of grain, their manger full of hay, and a good grooming.

At any rate Lester said, "When I was a young guy, I would lay in wait with my prize possession, my Red Rider BB gun. When the last mules were coming up to go into the barn I would take aim and pull the trigger hittin' the biggest target I had - the rear end of the last mule."

As expected, the team bolted toward the barn. Their building momentum had the power to stampede through the doors and out the other side. The hired driver pulled the many reins and frantically tried to slow the mules.

"All of a sudden there was an awful bunch of cussing and yelling you ever heard," Lester roared. "Oh, I laughed."

Lester suddenly sobered as he remembered the old days. His blue eyes cast the sincerity of a lesson learned.

"After a few times of helpin' out, my dad figured out what was goin' on and I lost my BB gun for awhile. Plus I couldn't sit down very well either."

Swift country justice. A rear for a rear.

What's an impressionable young boy to do when he has a grandfather, father, and uncles, who all pull pranks on each other? Uncles Gene, Ernest, and Babe Freeman might not have considered they were examples of how to behave, yet they taught young Lester well.

"When I was little, my uncles used to clean the barns out there at Granddad's home ranch in Pleasant Valley. They dumped the horse manure down the canyon," Lester said and laughed. "Gene was the one who drove the team. After he emptied the manure out of the wagon he'd come like a bat outta hell runnin' the mules back to the barn. Ernest and Babe would close the barn door on 'im so they'd come runnin' around the corner and the door would be closed."

Although the mules avoided collision with the barn door, the tongue of the wagon didn't.

"They had to build a new door."

When the twins were boys of about eight years old, living with their family in Hog Canyon, they and their sisters attended Ellis School, the same one-room country schoolhouse their mother and father had attended.

By the time Lester and his siblings went to Ellis School, Clarence was a board member. The schoolhouse, itself, was the same but the location of it was not. It had been moved down the canyon, on a sled, to the small triangle shaped piece of ground at the corner of Hog Canyon Road and Ranchita Canyon Road.

ELLIS SCHOOLHOUSE

CHESTER ROUGEOT, DON STEWART,
LESTER ROUGEOT, AND ELMER WELLS AT ELLIS SCHOOL

"It doesn't look like enough room for it, but there it was, right on the corner there, by the crick." Lester remembered, "Somebody burned it down around 1960."

During the early 1930s, when the country was in the midst of the Great Depression, the twins were given more and more duties. It was typical for Lester to accompany his dad and Chester to help his mom.

"Chester was more of an indoor person, he liked flowers and the finer things in life," Lester said and then admitted, "I was the renegade."

On one such day, Lester remembered a roundup and branding at the Gottfried Ranch. Known today as the Heritage ranch, the Gottfried was a fourteen thousand (14,000) acre ranch that Lester's grandfather, Rega Freeman, leased to run cattle. Lester and his dad went to help. Whenever cowboy activities took place, it was excitement Lester didn't want to miss.

First thing that morning Lester was sent to milk a cow in the Gottfried barn. He was to take a pail, fill it with milk, and bring it back so the crew could have it for their coffee.

Of course, Lester did as he was told. All gangly limbs and ambitious confidence he strode across the yard to the barn, pail swinging to his side. Alongside the cow he sat and aimed a rhythmic and metallic beat of milk inside the pail. Practiced at milking, Lester was quite efficient at the task. With gusto he squeezed those teats until there was no more.

Unfortunately, cows aren't always the most graceful animals on the planet. Before Lester could pick up the pail, the cow managed to kick it over and spill all the milk.

Oh, great, he thought. Now what?

Knowing the cow was already milked out, Lester had to think fast in order to get the job done. He looked around.

Hey, why not? It's worth a try.

In an effort to fulfill his duty as the designated milk boy, Lester decided to tap into another source. About to make a wonderful discovery, he turned to a lactating mare.

Evidently the horse didn't mind being milked by Lester. If she had he might never have found out and marveled at the fact that each of a mare's two teats has not one, but two, sometimes three, orifices.

To this day it makes Lester burst out in uproarious laughter. Although he managed to hit the pail with one of the spouts, the other squirted milk in every direction.

Nevertheless, his job was accomplished. Lester was able to strut back across the yard with the frothy white liquid for the hardy hands to enjoy. There was only one problem. They didn't.

Turned out mare's milk tasted nothing like cow's milk. When questioned about his comeuppance Lester said there weren't any. Although he did mention, "They had no sense of humor."

Tough crowd.

As an example of his parents trust in Lester's capabilities, weekday mornings he was the designated buggy driver that took his siblings to school. Along the four mile route he stopped at neighboring ranches. At various times upward of fifteen different children had been transported to school in the Rougeot's buggy, including the Rougeots, the Stewarts, the Von Dollens, the Wells, and the Work children.

LESTER ROUGEOT DRIVES THE WELLS CHILDREN TO SCHOOL

"We rode horseback until my dad bought a buggy. We weren't allowed to race the horses at school," Lester revealed then laughed. "One day, Doris Von Dollen and I got into a race during lunch. I won because I could turn my horse around and be back across the bridge and Doris' horse would just keep goin'."

With no available things like the 2012 iPads for entertainment, no internet, no texting, or video chatting with their friends, the children had to find something to do in the mid 1930's. Luckily Lester was never lacking in ideas and ways to have fun. His imagination ran overtime, especially when it came to instigating excitement.

"Another time, we found an old tire on the way to school and tied it to the back of the buggy. One of us would hop on the tire and the driver, me, would take off down the road going as fast as we could. We ran into just one problem - the rope would break."

Instead of rope, which didn't prove strong enough to sustain the dragging of successive tire-riding children on wild rides, the children found something that was tough enough – barbed wire.

"Our little game went along real well until one day when we were out exercisin' the buggy horse at full speed," Lester confesses. "We came around a curve and met Bob Works, who ended up swervin' his car to miss me and the young man sittin' on the tire behind the buggy hanging on for dear life. Bob went straight to my dad and told on us so our tire riding days came to an abrupt halt."

JAKE TULEY'S HARVESTER

Over the years, there were many memorable things that happened on the roads near Lester's childhood home. Near the ranch on the east side of Hog Canyon Road, neighbor Jake Tuley had an incident at one of his grain fields.

HARVESTER WRECK – HOG CANYON ROAD ABOVE

"In that field above the road there, Jake's harvester broke free from its mule team," Lester told and pointed up a steep slope, more cliff like than hillside.

Though the mule's remained up above, the heavy equipment rolled through the fence, off the edge of the field, and over the cliff. It plummeted onto Hog Canyon Road, bounced across, and crashed into the gully on the other side. The wooden harvester splintered into nothing more than kindling on impact. The unsalvageable wreckage was a total loss at a time when a farmer needed his equipment most. To drive by and see the haphazard pile of sticks left an impression on Lester.

"I'll never forget it. My dad farmed that field right over there," Lester informed. He pointed across the gully where the harvester had crashed. "My parents went by here about fifteen minutes after it happened and went back home for the camera."

Headed north on Hog Canyon Road, the pavement wound around the oak dotted hills. Past Jake Tuley's harvester wreckage was the Foley Place, where Lester and his family lived.

"Right up that canyon there used to be some of the best dove shootin'," Lester blurted as his son Chester's pickup rolled along at sightseeing speed. "There was a spring back up in there. They used to come from Oakland down here to shoot doves. They'd take 'em up there and they'd cook a big dinner and sell it in the restaurants up there. They made out like bandits."

Also to the west side of Hog Canyon Road there stands a windmill.

"That windmill has the name Shorty Rougeot written on it," Lester said. Though Lester is the one who was given the nickname "Shorty", for reasons unknown, his father, Clarence, who had the nickname "Stub", must have signed his name Shorty Rougeot.

SNOW IN HOG CANYON

42

HOG CANYON SNOW STORM

During winter, the area was prone to cold and frost, but many years could pass between brief snowfalls. Just north of the corner where Jake Tuley's harvester wrecked, where Lester and his family lived, a rare snowstorm blew through one winter and changed everything.

Snowflakes floated in silence and soon the canyons, the fields, the tops of the fences, and the backs of the livestock were blanketed in white. Though it didn't last long, the land Lester knew so well had become unfamiliar. Transformed into a winter wonderland, such a seldom seen phenomenon was one of the simplest, most natural thrills children and adults could have experienced.

Though Lester enjoyed the memory of snow, he didn't like to think about December of 1935. But for the sake of documentation, he shared the story of how, after a long hard day in San Luis Obispo, Lester's mother, Thelma, drove the many miles home to Hog Canyon.

"It was December 24, 1935, Christmas time," Lester said. Distracted by the task at hand, Thelma's normal holiday spirit was nowhere to be found. Neither cheerful nor even a tiny bit jolly, there was nothing, not even a merry Christmas carol that could bring a smile to her lips.

As tears streaked her pale face, she searched for and found

her shovel. Although no one was around to see her, she snuck into the yard wearing her dress, hose, and shoes. Thelma counted her paces. She walked toward an almond tree until she found the right spot and tried to thrust the shovel into the cold and hardened winter soil. With the long wooden handle held in both hands she placed her foot on the top of the spade and pushed the tip into the earth.

Little by little she scooped up dirt and poured it to the side. Each shovel full of soil heavier and more burdensome than the last, she thought of the three of her children that she'd just taken that morning, as per doctor's orders, to the children's ward at General Hospital on Johnson Road in San Luis Obispo.

Unlike the freedom of the farm the Rougeot children were confined to a place where there were no fragrant fields, no wildlife, and no winter sunshine to warm their cherubic cheeks. Instead there were sterile white sheets and walls, medicinal odors, and the unfamiliar sounds of monitors and serious staff when there should have been traditional songs to sing and gifts to wrap.

Alas, Christmas was the last thing on Thelma's mind. Again and again she removed soil from the hole until she heard the metal tip of the spade scrape the metal can she had hidden in the ground. When she tossed the shovel aside she dropped to her knees. Unconcerned by the damage she might cause to her good clothes, she leaned forward and began to dig with her hands. Cold dirt caked under her fingernails and her wedding ring as she pulled the old coffee can from its secret spot.

She searched every corner of her mind for ways to keep Lester and his sisters alive. She knew all too well that diphtheria could be fatal. Her gut wrenched.

"My twin brother, Chester, had already been in the hospital for two weeks," Lester recalled. "He'd died just the day before."

In the throes of heartache, Thelma felt she could not bear the pain a second time.

As she lifted the can and swiped away dirt from the outside of it, she vowed she would never again bury money. That way, she reasoned, she would never again have to unearth any to bury another loved one.

Though merry they were not, Clarence and Thelma were determined not to turn their backs on the needs of their surviving children.

"When we got out of the hospital," Lester recalled, "my parents had Christmas for us."

CHESTER ROUGEOT
JULY 20, 1925 – DECEMBER 24, 1935

3 – THE LONE TWIN

"When Chester died there was a big void," Lester said. For a ten year old survivor twin, who not only came home from the hospital, but never even contracted diphtheria, any feelings besides emptiness remained unidentified. Instead Lester internalized whatever guilt, or loneliness, or sorrow he may have experienced.

Surrounded by family, yet for the first time in his life a lone twin, no one felt Chester's absence more than Lester. From the moment of conception the boys had shared, explored, competed, and taken each other into consideration in their day to day lives. Although Lester claimed they "spared" in the womb and had very different personalities and preferences, the boys were 'the twins' – a package deal. Yet, never again would his blonde haired brother be there at the breakfast table, in the classroom, or just there every time Lester turned around. Never again would the twins be together to celebrate their birthday.

Sure, Lester would heal from the loss of his twin, but he'd forever be changed. A permanent loss, somewhat like an amputation of a body part, like part of a foot where the loss can be concealed inside a shoe, after the amputee relearns how to maneuver in the world, after they appear to be balanced and stable, others assume everything is back to normal. What people couldn't see was the underlying grief that was neither discussed nor defined but rather endured.

Of course everyone in the family coped with the loss in their own way and according to their own time frame. Nevertheless, life on the farm demanded that one foot be put in front of the other no matter how much a person may have wanted to stay hidden under the covers. Odd as it may have seemed, life went on without Chester.

For the next couple years, through the sixth grade, Lester continued to drive the buggy full of children to Ellis School, just as he had when Chester was alive.

Traveling to school and to his Grandparents by horseback, by buggy, and by car Lester learned the roads so well he may have been able to traverse them blindfolded.

Past the many acres along Von Dollen and Hog Canyon Roads where Lester's father, Clarence, farmed, the landscape that in 2012 is covered in straight rows of grape vines was, at that time, 1936, rolling hills and fields abound in grain. Healthy green shoots of graceful wheat and barley in the spring and stout golden stalks during the summer. During harvest season those hills were literally crawling with mule teams and hardworking crews.

CLARENCE ROUGEOT DRIVES MULE TEAM
IN PIONEER DAY PARADE 1936

"They used those old harvesters 'til the late thirties. Dad got a tractor and the next year I pulled the harvester with the tractor," Lester said. "At the Pioneer Day Parade, Dad used my granddad's mules, five abreast, to pull the harvester down the street, and some Jewish people saw the mules. After the parade they asked if the mules were for sale. By then I'd already started to lead the team back to the ranch." Eleven year old Lester rode a horse and led the string of mules from the streets of Paso Robles out toward his grandfather Freeman's on Von Dollen Road. He'd made it as far as an oak tree on Tower Road, which connects Airport and Jardine Roads, before his grandfather caught up to him and made the sale right under the tree. Lester then led the mules to the ranch and the buyers picked them up another day.

Left - LESTER ROUGEOT - 1937
Right - MART TAYLOR LIFTS LESTER -1937

After Ellis School, Lester attended Pleasant Valley School for the seventh grade. He and his family had moved from the Foley place to the Byer's place nearby. The family had purchased four thousand acres of land in Indian Valley in 1937 but could not reside there until 1938. They lived at the Byer Place, located on Lester's Grandfather Freeman's ranch, in the interim.

"When we bought the ranch in Indian Valley, it was seven or eight dollars an acre for the bottom land," Lester recalled, "and ten dollars an acre for the hills."

Soon after taking possession of the Indian Valley Ranch, Lester started the eighth grade in the one room schoolhouse down the road.

INDIAN VALLEY SCHOOLHOUSE
COURTESY ALBERTA BONNIFIELD

"Indian Valley School is over a hundred years old," Lester informed as he stood in front of the abandoned structure in February 2012. He walked and looked around to the side spotting a well. "We had to haul water to the school. At that time there was no well."

LESTER ROUGEOT AT INDIAN VALLEY SCHOOLHOUSE
FEBRUARY 2012

"They call this Big Sandy Creek," Lester said. "There's no water in it now, but when there's a good rain, the water would go so fast we wouldn't ride a horse in it. Pigs and horses can swim good but, they'd have a hard time gettin' across."

After a substantial rainfall, the wide creek bed was known to fill with water that roared down the canyon. Up Big Sandy Creek where the country becomes more wooded, hilly, and desolate, the terrain is covered in a variety of vegetation. Over the decades three generations of Rougeots harvested their Christmas trees there and gathered pinecones to help start their fires.

The lore of Stone Canyon Coal Mine, up the road in the nearby mountains, held a certain fascination for Lester. No longer in operation when his immediate family moved to Indian Valley in 1938, there were remnants, such as sections of the railroad, that could be, and still can be, seen alongside parts of Indian Valley Road where Lester stated, "Back in the 1920's there used to be a saloon."

According to Lester, the railroad was built with mule teams and Fresno scrapers. A train hauled coal from the mine to a dump site just north of San Miguel at the McKay Station, before being transported to San Francisco. Years later, the Rougeot family had to buy a couple miles of the railroad track that ran through their property. Though the tracks, themselves, were useless to either the railroad company or the Rougeot's, the family paid fifty dollars an acre.

"Indians told the miners when they first started minin' the coal that the mine would catch on fire and they'd have to let the water loose in there to put it out," Lester told. "And by golly, that's exactly what happened." As the story goes, there was a source of water right at the top of the mine that was let loose to douse the fire.

The coal, according to Lester, wasn't old enough and had too much sulfur in it. Although the mine was closed by then, Lester's grandfather had leased land in the area so family had access to leftover coal.

"If you tried to use it in a forge it would smoke," Lester said. "Daddy put some in the cookstove for Momma to use one day and it blew the lids off the stove."

In an area known to locals as "the breaks", a deep canyon with mountains on either side, there were reportedly petrified clam shells.

"There were layers of them," Lester remembered, "like they were in cement."

The clam site was a favored field trip for Indian Valley School students back when Lester was thirteen.

"My dad took the boys and the teacher took the girls," he said. "Later, there were roads built but, at the time, we walked down a cow trail into the canyon to see them."

As told by Lester, it was be a bit of a hike to get back in there and Clarence, Lester's dad, was concerned the students might want to take a drink from the spring when they got there. Lester remembered his dad lecturing the boys.

"I want to tell you kids somethin'," Clarence said to get their attention. "Don't you drink any of that water up there 'cause it'll make you shit like a loose goose."

Well, that warning was taken to heart by one of the boys, Bobby Cole. He was anxious to share the advice with the teacher and the girls. As soon as the boys' and girls' vehicles arrived at the head of the trail, Bobby jumped out of the boys' car and ran over to the teacher who was getting out of the girls' car. Try as he might to get the words out, Bobby's excitement exaggerated his speech impediment.

As Clarence and the rest of the boys caught up with Bobby they heard him stutter out his words of caution, "Mi-Mi-Miss Burke, Mi-Mi-Mister Rougeot says na-na-not to dri-dri-drink any of the wa-wa-water 'cause you'll sh-sh-shit like a loose goose."

A look of astonishment crossed Miss Burke's face just before she threw her hand over her gaping mouth. Lester recalled uproarious laughter from the group of children as his dad attempted to contain his own.

THE ROUGEOT RANCH - INDIAN VALLEY 1940

Lester was often off with his father, Clarence. It was a time when coyotes were, and in many places still are, considered pests, as worthless and bothersome as ground squirrels, maybe worse. Squirrels caused damage to the crops and the agricultural fields. Coyotes killed chickens and barn cats. They fought with ranch dogs and dug horse-crippling holes. Farmers and ranchers shot squirrels and coyotes on sight. Sometimes they poisoned them.

CLARENCE ROUGEOT – INDIAN VALLEY 1940

On one particular day, when Lester and Clarence were riding in the hills and had no gun with them, they saw a coyote.

"We were movin' forty head of horses from the Gottfried Ranch, which is now known as the Heritage Ranch, to Indian Valley," Lester remembered. "Dad had a good stallion. He used him to breed horses for the neighbors. When the water got low at the Heritage Ranch we'd trail 'em to the home ranch. We'd take the horses across the Old Nacimiento Ranch, which is Camp Roberts, and go across the Salinas River. But if we were movin' cattle from the Gottfried, we'd go underneath the San Marcos Bridge, across the Salinas River. It'd take two days 'cause we'd take 'em clear to Grandpa Freeman's home ranch in Estrella. We'd make it to Mustang Springs with the cows and calves, stay overnight, then the next day we'd take 'em clear to the Pleasant Valley Ranch between Hog Canyon and Ranchita Canyon."

"Any ways, when we was movin' these horses this one time, we saw a coyote. My dad took off after it."

Clarence encouraged his horse into a run. At high speed the horse quickly gained on the coyote. When Clarence was in range, he roped it, jumped off his horse, and slammed the coyote to the ground.

"I was afraid he'd get bit," Lester said. "But it didn't fight. It cowered." Lester sat on his horse and watched as his dad picked up a rock and killed the coyote.

For Lester, Indian Valley was better than an amusement park. A gregarious young teenager, when the family first settled there, he quickly bonded with the land as well as the people.

Marion and Alberta Bonnifield were neighbors of the Rougeots in the late 1930's. Currently, in 2012, Alberta resides at the same ranch she and Marion built in their younger years.

A strong-willed and capable ranch woman, Alberta said, "I dug all the post holes for the fences with Marion. And we built all the barns and sheds ourselves."

"All of Alberta and Marion's animals were like pets," Lester's son, Chester remembered. "Even the cows were tame. You could walk out among 'em, no problem."

ALBERTA BONNIFIELD AND LESTER ROUGEOT 2012

Several times over the years Alberta had been asked by Fish and Game authorities if she would like to take on an orphaned fawn, which she agreed to do. Even today she has a full grown doe in her yard, which is protected from predators by a high fence and a readily available loaded .410 shotgun.

"I let the kid (the deer) in the house once in awhile," Alberta said and laughed. "Not for very long though 'cause I'm afraid she'll pee on my carpet."

Friends for some sixty years, Alberta and Lester were at ease in each other's company as the gracious hostess, Alberta offered coffee and cookies in her kitchen. They reminisced about events of years gone by and talked of things that concerned ranchers and farmers, such as rain totals, predators, and poachers.

LESTER ROUGEOT AND CLARENCE ROUGEOT
INDIAN VALLEY 1941

Although much of Alberta and Marion Bonnifield's original ranch eventually sold, after Marion's passing, Alberta kept the two houses, the barns, and sheds – which along with all the fencing are all in great shape to this day, not to mention immaculate.

FRANCIS MCKANNA AND MARION BONNIFIELD
COURTESY MELBA MCKANNA

Another Indian Valley neighbor of the Rougeot's, Merle Ferris, piped drinking water from a sand stone cave, and allowed neighbors to come and fill their buckets and barrels with his water. Unlike many of the water sources in Indian Valley, which Lester described as alkaline and tasted nasty, Merle's water was sweet and refreshing.

"Merle and his dad had an egg ranch, which had a truck from Paso Robles come out to pick up their eggs once a week," Lester said. "Bud Barba's the one who drove the Dadar's truck out there from town to pick up the eggs."

Merle Ferris lived there when Lester was young and was still there when Lester's son, Chester, lived there in the 1970's.

"I remember going to Merle's with Marion Bonnifield. Marion took a fifty-five gallon barrel to fill. I took five gallon buckets," Chester told.

"Down the canyon," Lester said, "another neighbor, Leo Ferris, used slabs of local jasper to build his structures."

Though Indian Valley Road was, and is, a very rural road, there were times during the year, such as deer hunting season, when it was more traveled than others.

"You know, they talk about these dry land watermelons? Well, we planted those back in the 1930's up at the ranch in Indian Valley. Us kids, during deer season, would take and put up a stand out there by the road under this big old oak tree and sell watermelons to the deer hunters for two bits a piece.

"Everybody that drove by and saw our sign stopped by and got a watermelon," Lester remembered. Enterprising from a young age Lester tested his salesmanship skills at a road side stand his sisters and he had set up. A makeshift table with a homemade sign and a wagon full of melons hauled out to their mini farmer's market was a profitable project for the children."

Of course the children had their fill of watermelon too. "We had so damn many of 'em we'd take a wagon down there and fill it up with watermelons and throw 'em in for the pigs. We never had to worry about spittin' seeds 'cause we'd just take and cut the heart out of 'em and eat that."

Older, and trusted by his parents to be out on his own, Lester hunted, fished, and explored every nook and cranny of the nearby canyons. It was in effect, the place Lester grew into a man.

Lester's father, Clarence, must have considered him a young man by that time as well. After Lester graduated from Indian Valley School's 1938 eighth grade class, Clarence, who himself had gone on to college for a year, put a very adult decision squarely in Lester's lap.

"You decide, son, if you'd like to further your education in high school or not," Clarence had said. "It's up to you."

And yes, Lester did want to go to Paso Robles High School.

"My sister, Gladys, and I drove sixteen miles from the ranch to the railroad tracks in San Miguel," Lester recalled. "Then we caught the bus to Paso Robles High School every day."

Paso Robles High School had just begun a program that, along with all the pretty girls, Lester was very interested in. The program was the Future Farmers of America, F.F.A..

"While I attended Paso Robles High School I became a Charter member of the Future Farmers of America in 1939," Lester stated. It was his freshman year.

The agricultural program was a place for Lester to showcase his talents and experience success. Straight off the farm he took on projects where he would excel. In addition to agriculture classes and the required curriculum, Lester learned to weld, took wood shop, and automobile shop classes - which he particularly enjoyed in part because of the underground mechanics pit from where he could view any girls who were above.

F.F.A. sponsored many contests for students in agriculture. One particular competition was evaluating and scoring dairy cows.

"Don Stewart and I, we went to high school together too, we was both in F.F.A. For the dairyman's contest they sent out these pictures to judge these cows. So one day at noon we decided hell we got time. Let's go judge these cows. So we went in there and marked those cows. I think there was only one cow that him and I had different. But I scored high in the nation. So, anyway, they sent me the other papers to give my reasons. Well, the ag teacher there said, 'You're gonna do this.' So durin' class I was workin' on them cows. Well, sent it all in and when it come back I'd won third place in the nation. The prize was ten dollars," Lester stated then exclaimed, "All that work for ten dollars!" Countless hours of paperwork wasn't Lester's thing.

"In 1941 and 1942 Paso Robles had a fair across from where Robbins Field is now," Lester remembered. The town boasted around three thousand residents back in those days. "We had set up holding pens in the vacant lot. Kenny Kester from Shandon had Angus and took all the awards in that class. I showed Herefords and took all of the awards in that class." Lester laughed as he told how Kenny and he had proudly won all the ribbons. Never mind they were the only two contestants.

BLUE, RED, BLUE - 1942

During his senior year, 1942/43, Lester served as president of the F.F.A. Turned out Lester excelled at leadership as well as showmanship. But that wasn't all he aimed his sights on.

"When I was in high school I bought my .22 pistol from Tom Brown in Bradley for fifty dollars. It's a .22 Colt revolver on a .38 frame," Lester stated. "I could shoot a fly with that thing."

According to Lester, the handy firearm, was light weight and accurate. Seems that pistol was packed around with him at all times.

"I shot a buzzard outta the sky one time. I was on the back porch and I pulled out my pistol. It fell in the chicken yard." Although the big black bird wasn't dead, Lester had shot it in the wing; he remembered the bird's unpleasant odor. "That thing smelled like hell. Oh, my dad was mad."

Seems Lester upset more than just his dad by using his pistol. One day brother-in-law, Johnny Craspay, made the mistake of spouting off about how Lester couldn't shoot the small ball (about the size of a fly) off the antennae of Johnny's car.

"Hell, he said I couldn't do it," Lester said in an exasperated tone. "What was I supposed to do? Oh, he was pissed."

During deer season, Lester remembered hunting with the game warden. "We both got our limit," Lester said. "It was during the war and shells were hard to get. Every time they came up they brought a carton of .22 shells."

Scarce ammunition or not, Lester was always armed and ready for action.

"I was horseback one time and I chased this buck about two hundred fifty yards and it got winded," Lester said. "I shot it in the head with my pistol. I caught hell for that."

The Rougeot's not only hunted with wildlife authorities they participated in their programs as well.

"The Department of Fish and Game put in quail guzzlers out on the ranch when I was about seventeen," Lester remembered. "They did it there on the ranch 'cause my dad raised birds. He had quail, chukar, pheasant, and doves in pens. We ate some of 'em. It was a hobby for my dad. And King City and Bradley's forestry stations used to train firefighters how to make a fire break in the brush up at the ranch in Indian Valley too. Dad used to get a lot of brush cleaned up for free that way."

A life filled with outdoor activities held its appeal, but hunting dove and deer wasn't the only thing Lester pursued. As far as social events went, he said he liked dances. Though he had never been taught, he watched others from the side line and eventually got up the nerve to ask a girl to dance.

"Kitty Belle Curtis, I'll never forget," Lester announced. "She was a jolly gal from the valley and my first, ever, dance partner. I had so much fun."

When in high school Lester and another local Indian Valley girl, Violet Rose, Alberta Bonnifield's sister, put on dances. "Violet started the dances," Lester recalled. "I helped." Those dances were held at the Indian Valley one-room schoolhouse.

"We had this one dance called, 'The Paul Jones'," Lester remembered. "It was live music and everybody'd be dancin' and everybody'd make a circle and hold hands. Well, the women went to the right and the men to the left and vice versa then when you felt like ya wanted to dance again you hollered, 'Paul Jones,' and whoever's was right there, you'd dance with 'em. Then you'd dance that out and they'd say everybody join hands and you'd have three or four partners every dance."

"It's kinda like musical chairs," Lester's son Chester described.

"I'll never forget this one time when Charles Burden had brought this Emery girl," Lester recalled. "Oh, she was cute as a bug's ear."

"One of those Emery girls was Miss California, ya know," Alberta Bonnifield recounted. "They were beautiful girls."

"So Francis McKanna and I decided we was gonna take her away from Charles," Lester continued. "And we did."

"Well, you ornery devil," Alberta exclaimed.

"Well, we was just havin' fun," Lester excused and laughed. "Francis and I were always hollerin', 'Paul Jones,' when we got to her and Charles was with somebody else. He had no sense of humor. He got so mad he took 'er home."

When Lester and Francis got together there always seemed to be a lot of laughs - at least for them. "Francis' mom and my mom were best friends," Lester said as he revisited the old days.

"Oh, I never will forget the night that Bob Work come out there to the schoolhouse and brought a case of half pint bottles of whiskey. And they took ol' Shorty Wiedaman out there to get 'im a drink, you know. So ol' Shorty he just took the lid off one of those bottles and tipped it up, drank the whole thing, and threw this bottle over the fence. Nobody else got a drink out of it. He'd get so drunk he'd be passed out sittin' there blowin' his horn. Asleep."

Although people from all over the area danced seemingly without a care, it was a turbulent time for America. The 1941 attack on Pearl Harbor brought the country into World War II. Local boys left for military service. The Pacific coast was on alert. Residences, businesses, and vehicles had to be able to "black out" windows and headlights so that enemy bombers would have no lights to aim at. Californians and others who resided on the Pacific coast truly feared Japanese air raids on the mainland. A Japanese submarine had already sunk an oil tanker off the coast of Cambria. War wasn't just thousands of miles away, it was in the neighborhood.

Camp Roberts, the closest military reservation to Lester's home, had transformed the Old Nacimiento Ranch's grazing ground into training grounds. For the next few years, troops would prepare for war right in Lester's back yard. And still the people danced, and worked, and went to school.

"Granddad Freeman helped me get my State Farmer Degree and they wanted me to go on for the national but I said, 'Bull, I ain't gonna keep all them records in another damn book for all that stuff just to get a piece of paper."

The undertaking that produced results more to Lester's liking - his steer project.

"As my ag project for State F.F.A. Degree, I fed out seventy steers for ninety days. The steers had Granddad Freeman's brand on 'em. He owned 'em and sold 'em to me. We fixed up a deal that was legitimate but no money changed hands."

FREEMAN RANCH
LOCATED ON VON DOLLEN ROAD BETWEEN RANCHITA CANYON
AND HOG CANYON IN THE PLEASANT VALLEY AREA

The barn at the Freeman's Von Dollen Road Ranch was where Lester fed his seventy steers their daily rations of chopped oat hay, ground barley, cotton seed meal, and molasses.

"We bought loose oat hay, in other words it wasn't baled, and it was hauled from the Quenser place by a team and wagon up to my granddad's place and run through a Case chopper into this barn. We had scales there too 'cause my granddad bought the scales from the old Nacimiento Ranch and put in out there at the ranch."

Not only did Lester keep track of his herd's weight gain on those scales - an impressive three pounds per day per steer - he was also known to set up the welding equipment and make repairs on that metal contraption.

"Nowadays they feed fancy stuff and can't even get two pounds per day," Lester marveled. "I got up early enough to feed the steers before school and then again in the evening. At the end of the ninety days I sold those steers and made a profit of two thousand dollars." It was a tidy sum for anyone, let alone a teenager. In 2012 dollars a two thousand dollar ($2,000.00) profit would be worth between twenty-six and twenty-seven thousand dollars ($26,000.00 - $27,000.00).

Lester spent much time with his grandparents, Rega and Dovie Freeman. In fact, he lived with them during his senior year.

REGA AND DOVIE FREEMAN

"Granddad would come pick me up at school and we'd go to the ranch up there in San Ardo and I'd fix whatever he needed fixed like the windmill tower, the sucker rods, and he'd be in the pickup holdin' the light for me."

Since it was after school, often it would be dark when doing the chores. Lester remembered fixing the water tower sucker rods, forty feet off the ground with nothing more than the beam of a spotlight to see by.

"This was in the forties," Lester said. "Granddad and I stayed in the bunkhouse this one night and he says, 'You know, Les, I've got about six hundred thousand dollars in these ranches', that was with the cattle and all."

According to the United States Bureau of Labor Statistics that six hundred thousand dollars ($600,000.00) would have the buying power of seven million eight hundred thirty-four thousand six hundred two dollars and twenty-seven cents ($7,834,602.27) in 2012. No surprise that about that time, Rega felt solvent enough to consider making another land purchase. However, Rega knew if he were to travel in search of land, he would have to count on others to take care of the chores at home. That was something he wasn't sure he could do without wondering if things were getting done, or not.

THE FREEMAN FAMILY

"Granddad would send his sons or nephews to take care of, you know, work for 'im at his Red Head Ranch but they'd never stay and get it done," Lester began. "He called the ranch in San Ardo, out Red Head Canyon, his Hoodoo Ranch. His kids had a chance to take it over but they took off."

It was typical practice to name one's ranch. Often a ranch would be called by its original owner's name, the current owner's name, or its geographic location. But the naming of Rega's Hoodoo Ranch was none of those. The only possible clue, or simply a coincidence, in regards to where he might have come up with the name – there was a notorious outlaw called 'Hoodoo Brown' who had been run out of New Mexico into Texas, in 1880, a time when Rega was just a child living in the lone star state.

THE FREEMAN FAMILY – 1939

TOP ROW – BABE, GENE, THELMA FREEMAN ROUGEOT, THOMAS RICHARD, AND ERNEST
BOTTOM ROW – MARGARET, DOVIE, REGA, ONA

"Granddad said, 'You know, Les you're the only one who ever started a job up here and finished it'," Lester stated. "I helped build the corral up there. I spent two weeks, on my own, alone, while puttin' up the hay. The water was alkaline, terrible to drink. And rattlesnakes, it wasn't unusual to kill five a day. Granddad's Red Head Ranch was four thousand acres. He ran more cattle there than the Gottfried Ranch, now the Heritage Ranch, which was fourteen thousand acres, that he rented. There was no water at the Gottfried Ranch until they had the dam in there for Nacimiento. In the summer time, you'd pump the well dry in a few hours then you'd have to leave it sit."

A high school senior in 1942/43 Lester was aware of the war but, for the most part, unworried. Of far more importance in Lester's life were school, work, and girls. Not necessarily in that order. Girls were a main attraction for Lester. Though he felt he'd outgrown his innocence, his know-how would soon be tested.

Although Lester claimed that just a few short years earlier, "I was just a kid from the hills who thought girls were just a bunch lumpy boys," Lester asserted, "by high school I had it figured out." But, did he?

"A girl from school locked me in the shop supply cage with her," Lester remembered. He was a senior when the bold high school freshman, Norma Botts, cornered him. It was his big chance to find out something first hand.

Norma moved toward him. So close was Norma that Lester could have felt her breath or smelled her shampoo - opportunity stared him in the face. What did he do? He froze. No kiss, no fondle, no nothing - except for awkwardness and laughter. "The room had wire walls. There were other students outside pointin' and laughin'," Lester defended and claimed with a chuckle, "I knew what it was all about. I just didn't know what to do with it."

Better stick with dancing.

He did. For Lester's senior prom, especially for the occasion, his parents bought him a new suit.

That was right about the same time Lester bought himself a saddle. "Vic Palm picked me up at the Paso Robles High School and took me to the Paso Robles Mercantile," Lester recalled. "A new Keystone, handmade western saddle had come in at the store and I wanted to see it." Lester looked it over, liked it, and made the purchase. He'd saved for his own saddle by working harvests and doing handyman ranch work around the valley in addition to his most profitable steer project. It was 1943, and Lester, the young cowboy and horse trainer, finally had his own saddle.

Not long after that purchase, Lester, along with Norm Bridge, Donna Dusey, Marilyn Palla (McWilliams), Janie Ransky, Beverly Lyle (Tornquist) graduated from the ivy covered brick Paso Robles high school.

The year after his high school graduation, Lester received an official looking letter in the mail. "I got called up in 1944," Lester said. It was war time and he, along with others in the area, received papers that gave them instructions of where to go in San Francisco to be examined. "A bunch of us went up on a Greyhound bus. I passed the physical and come home and the family doctor, Dr. L. Strahan, had got me deferred on account of my dad. He knew my dad's condition, a bad heart, and we had the ranch up there. I don't know how he did it, but I didn't have to go." Not only did Clarence depend on Lester to help on the ranch, it wouldn't have been fair to Thelma who had already lost Lester's twin, Chester. Neither parent could afford to lose another son to war or anything else.

In any case Lester dodged the bullets of war. Or, more likely, the enemy had dodged his. Regardless, military service was not an experience Lester and his parents would have to suffer through. No combat for Lester, no anguish for Thelma.

Though school was out, Lester's appetite for fun was still all in. On Sunday afternoons Lester and his good buddy, Francis McKanna were often at a river. Near the bridge that crossed the Salinas River in Bradley they had a favored fishing hole, as well as Santa Rita Creek to the south, and a section of the San Antonio River further north.

In order to set a time to meet with Francis, Lester would use the telephone, which at that time was a party line that his dad, Clarence, maintained. The Rougeot's party line had twelve neighboring families on the same line.

"Each house had its own ring, two shorts and one long ring, or something like that and you knew the call was for you." Even though each household had its own identifying ring seems people couldn't help themselves from picking up the receiver even when it wasn't a call for them. It was entertainment of sorts to listen in on someone else's call. And in Lester's case, when he and Dorothy Twisselman called to chat with each other, it was entertainment to mess with neighbors who eaves dropped. "Dorothy and I used to talk about the neighbors, tell stories, make stuff up. Man you ought to hear all the receivers go click, click, click."

At any rate, so as to avoid tipping off any busy-bodies that were on the line at the same time, Lester and Francis developed a code.

"The chickens are in," Francis would say. Lester would know the steelhead had come up the river and were abundant. The twosome would pack some supplies, usually in the form of VO whiskey, and set out to catch their limit.

FRANCIS MCKANNA AT THE ROUGEOT RANCH
IN INDIAN VALLEY
COURTESY OF MELBA MCKANNA

Though many fishermen would have used an official pole complete with line and hook, Lester and Francis had what they liked to call their "Portugue fly rod", a barbed spear. No line, no hook, no sinker.

In addition to their "Portugue" fishing gear, they sometimes used a pitchfork. Or, as with a fishing trip with Jim and Lou Schmidt, while fishing steelhead in a Nacimiento River tributary, "Jim stuck his .22 down in water by the fish and killed it," Lester recalled with a hoot. "Lou swam his horse out in the water in these holes and run the fish outta there and I'd stand on the bank shootin' 'em with my .3030. I got one fish with my .22. We got eight to ten steelhead."

Other times, the men fished with what Lester described as, "a frog gig." To catch a fish with a barbed spear meant they needed good aim and ample thrust. Although most expeditions they did manage to catch fish, there was a time when Francis chased after what turned out to be an eel. It was in the San Antonio River. Francis plunged his spear into the water and impaled what he thought was the eel. Wrong. Neither was it a fish that he had stabbed.

"Francis stabbed my foot. God Almighty, I'll never forget that. I just sat down in the water and pulled that thing out. It was the one with the spear on it. It had the little barb there to keep it from comin' out. Man it got big, my foot did. But I was drunk so it didn't bother me."

LESTER ROUGEOT ROPER ON RIGHT

Atop a horse he was training for a florist in San Luis Obispo named Tex Wilson, Lester rode all over the territory. A trip to the nearest town was a twelve mile ride to get supplies. The twenty-four mile round trip was part of his mount's training program.

On one such day, the ride across the countryside meant hours of solitude and quiet. The only company was an occasional ground squirrel, coyote, buzzard, or deer. The only sounds were the squeak of new saddle leather in time with hoof beats and an occasional hawk's cry.

A straw cowboy hat shaded Lester's face from the sun as his horse hoofed into town. The plan was to meet up with his friend, Francis McKanna, when he arrived in Bradley. Lester described Bradley as, 'a poke and clean town'. "You poke your head out the window and you're clean through town." Not much going on in Bradley – that is until Lester would show up to visit his buddy, Francis.

That was the day Lester decided he wanted some chewing gum. Being the good pal that he was, Francis was easily persuaded into helping Lester get that gum. Over to Al Rist's grocery store they went. When they arrived, Lester didn't bother to dismount or tie the horse to the hitching rail. Instead, he had Francis open the grocery store door as wide as it would swing.

Lester ducked his head on the way through the threshold and rode right up to the store's counter. Much to the surprise of Ella and Jean Rewirts, sisters who were working in the store that day, Lester sat on the horse, asked for chewing gum, dug into his pocket for money, and paid. Too small of an area to turn around, he then reined the horse into its reverse gear and out the door he went unsure if his and the horse's combined weight could break through the wooden board floor underneath them or not. Luckily, Lester and his horse backed out of the store and nothing terrible happened. Just some fodder for any gossip mongers who witnessed him clowning around.

As one might expect, after a long hot ride into town, Lester felt the rumblings of hunger. Evidently, the gum hadn't curbed his appetite for food, or fun.

"We headed to the restaurant to get a bite to eat," Lester said. But news traveled fast in a poke and clean town. Sure enough, word of Lester's antics had made its way next door faster than he had. When he and Francis tried to enter the establishment the door was locked.

"They didn't want me ridin' up the stairs."

No matter. Lester soon found somewhere else to get a meal and horse around.

"I'd ride horseback from the ranch in Indian Valley to Tom and Emily Freeman's," Lester remembered. Tom Freeman was Lester's second cousin, his mother, Thelma's uncle Joe Freeman's son.

"Tom and Emily's ranch is east of San Ardo. I'd leave home and ride on the county road about five miles then go left into the hills another three miles to get there. I knew where all the fences and gates were along the way." Had he stayed on the county road Lester would have also been able to claim he knew every inch of road from there to Parkfield.

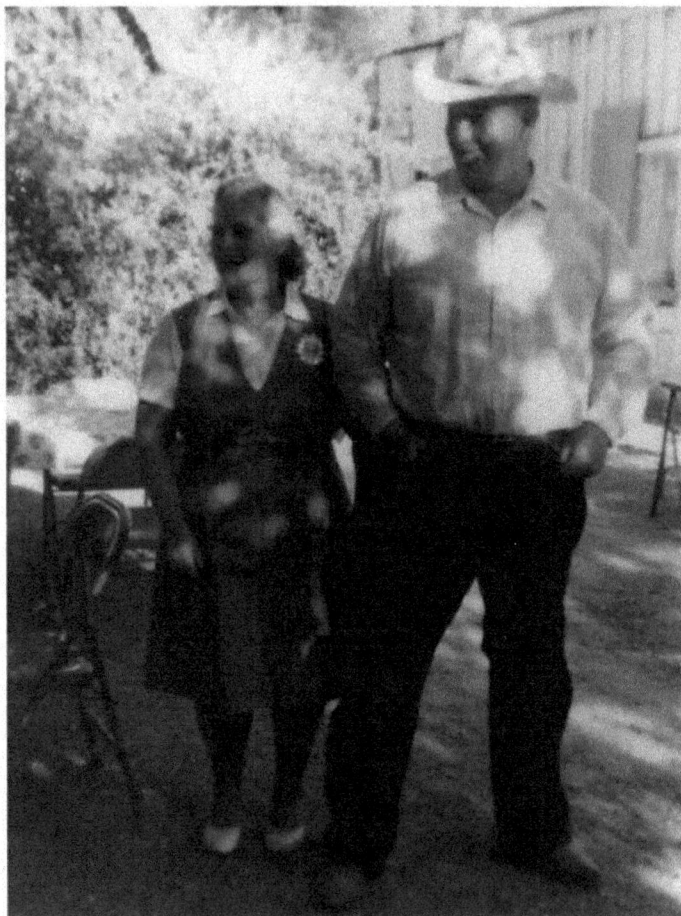

EMILY AND TOM FREEMAN – 25TH WEDDING ANNIVERSARY

"The County had sent us a dozer down there and a pull grader. I'd drive the dozer and my dad would run the grader and we'd grade the road into Parkfield, another twenty to twenty-five miles.

"I remember the time we was gradin' the road there at Tom and Emily Freeman's Ranch. I was runnin' the grader and someone was runnin' the tractor and we went over this kind of knoll and I just sank the grader blade down and the tractor couldn't pull it. It'd stand there and spin," Lester said. "I laughed like hell and my dad come over there and give me hell."

Besides pulling pranks when at the Tom and Emily Freeman Ranch, Lester was known to be helpful and entertaining. During the barley harvest, Lester liked to get a boost into the harvester. "I'd run up the tire to get up in there," Lester said. The rolling tire propelled him right up to the seat. If not physical labor or pranks, how about acrobatics? "I was real agile."

"Like a hamster on a wheel," Emily's nephew Paul Buren commented. Paul is the son of Charlotte, Emily Freeman's sister.

"There was this time when we were haulin' hay into the barn and Lester said he saw a buck," Emily Freeman recalled.

TOM FREEMAN - SAN ARDO FREEMAN RANCH

Folks who muscled around tons of hay, from one place to another, tended to develop a powerful hunger for protein. Tom and Lester had been hauling wagon loads of loose hay into the barn, using a system that utilized a horse, ropes, a metal track, a fork, and pulleys. Lester had been riding the horse that pulled the ropes when he informed Tom that he'd just seen dinner walk by.

"Emily come out of the house and took over for me," Lester said. "Only she walked the horse, I rode it 'cause I was lazy."

"We thought he was pullin' our leg to get out of work," Emily remembered and told how Lester went up the road with a rifle. When he had been out of sight for awhile, they assumed he was fooling around instead of working. That is until they heard the gun shot. "Before long, here comes Lester draggin' a deer with the hind feet over his shoulder." Emily laughed at the memory.

TOM FREEMAN – GROUND CREW FAR LEFT

After a hard day's work and a hearty meal, there was a song Lester liked to play on the Freeman's record player. Determined to learn every word, Lester played it over and over. "Tom had a record I listened to," Lester remembered. "It was *The Whole Damn Family*. I played it on an old Victrola. Played it every chance I got and damn near wore it out."

Seems the song *The Whole Damn Family* was not just a hit with Lester. It was so much fun to sing, and to hear, it became a song that several generations of Rougeots and Freemans were entertained by.

"I asked my grandma, mom, and aunt and they all remembered that my grandfather sang *The Whole Damn Family* all the time," Tom and Emily Freeman's granddaughter, Dusty Rossi said. "When I asked her about the song, my grandma quickly sang out the following, 'Old Man Damn, Old Miss Damn, and the whole Damn Family'. It's like Old Man Damn does something and Old Miss Damn does something, etcetera. My aunt, Joanne Errea, my Grandparent's oldest child, remembered my grandfather singing it all her life and my mom, Kathy Rossi, my grandparent's youngest, remembered him singing it a lot when they built fence and did other stuff. He had a lot of little songs and sayings that he used."

LESTER ROUGEOT AND STANLEY "BUD" BONNIFIELD

Singing songs, riding tires, shooting deer - the notion of fun can be very different among people from different backgrounds. Fun the country boy way was often border-line, if not downright, dangerous. Get a few cowboys together and there's bound to be some kind of Western entertainment on the horizon.

BUD BONNIFIELD

Much like his father and grandfather might have done for fun, there was a day Lester, along with friends Francis McKanna and Bud Bonnifield came up with an idea only cowboys could come up with. Being of similar minds, when the cattle buyer, Shorty Williams, showed up, he readily got onboard with the plan, as did Mary Orradre who had overheard the conversation. Mary told the men where to find a stash of wine there at the Orradre Ranch, and the group conspired to get Joe Ventura a glass - or two or three - to quench his thirst. One glass at a time, the scheme was to get Joe good and drunk.

REFRESHMENT CREW- BUD BONNIFIELD, FRANCIS MCKANNA AND LESTER ROUGEOT

The wine tasted delicious to Joe. He drank it down while joking around with the others as he proceeded to get comfortable on the front lawn.

"When he sat down, threw his feet in the air, and fell over backward," Lester said with a laugh, "we knew he was ready."

That's when Bud, a six feet four inch tall, long legged man, removed his chaps, strapped, and buckled them on Joe, also known as Little Joe, who had to hike them under his armpits. Bud then took his saddle off his horse. The stirrups were shortened. The motley crew then saddled up a seemingly docile Mexican steer.

"The next thing Little Joe knew, we'd picked 'im up, and stuck 'im on top of that steer." The men jumped back and the steer went off like fireworks. A few seconds later - thud. Little Joe hit the dirt. Although the dust didn't last much longer than the show, the story did. Cowboy entertainment can be tough. Luckily for Little Joe, he made it through the ordeal with no injuries.

"If he'd been sober it might have ended differently."

MILDRED "SIS" ROUGEOT AND LESTER ROUGEOT

Another day when Lester, Francis McKanna, and Stanley Bonnifield, also known as Bud, were at the Ventura Ranch, Joe's brother Johnny Ventura had a heifer he was moving inside a trailer. While Johnny wasn't looking or listening, the men, who had some extra time on their hands, talked about and decided they wanted to practice roping, to keep their skills up.

"Wouldn't you know it right about that time, Johnny's heifer escaped the trailer. Being the accommodatin' guys we were we roped that heifer for Johnny."

The men even loaded the alleged unruly runaway back in the trailer. "Johnny just couldn't figure out how she'd gotten out to begin with." Ever so helpful, the guys explained how she must have scrambled over the side. Funny how there was no evidence of hide nor hair on that trailer.

ORRADRE RANCH BRANDING IN BRADLEY

On yet another day in San Ardo, a hot day, Lester again went to the Orradre Ranch, this time to help gather cattle. As expected in the heat of the day, Mitch Orradre's cattle were next to the oil fields, down under the trees in the riverbed, where it was shady and cool. No matter how much Lester, Mitch, and Mitch's neighbor, Joe Ventura tried to move the cattle out from under those trees, the bovine just wouldn't budge. For some unknown reason the men didn't have any dogs with them that day or the dogs would have been in the brush nipping at the cows heels to get them to move.

Around and around the riverside brush the men went. They shouted and lunged their horses toward the cattle to no avail. Seeing their tactics were not going to work it didn't take Lester long before he came up with one of his plans.

Lester reined his horse over to Joe and asked, "Do you wanna make points with Mitch?"

"Well, yeah," Joe replied.

"Gi' me the end of your rope," Lester said.

Joe did as Lester commanded. That's when Lester took the end of Joe's lariat and tied it to a five gallon can. After he told Joe to dally the rope around his saddle horn Lester instructed him to run

77

down the bed of the creek with the attached can dragging behind him. The plan was to make enough noise with the can as it banged against rock that it would spook the cattle out of hiding. Once the herd was out from under the tangle of growth along the creek, the men could then gather them, then drive them back to the ranch.

With the can crashing behind Joe there was indeed racket enough to scare the bovine out of their shady spot. As the can beat creek rock, it banged loudly. The plan worked. There was only one problem. Every time the can and rope hit a bush, tree, or rock it bounced up and scared Joe's horse as well. This caused his horse to panic and take flight at a gallop. When the can snagged, it jerked Joe's arm so hard he lost his dally, which was probably a good thing since he needed both hands to hang on for dear life.

"That bucket would hit the ground and it'd jerk 'im back. I thought it was gonna jerk 'is arm off if he didn't let go," Lester said with wide eyes. "Joe's horse was out of control until it finally got to the fence."

Nevertheless, the men accomplished the job they set out to do, albeit the country boy way.

"When I was nineteen, Granddad Freeman, he'd gone up to northern California and looked at a ranch along the Eel River in Trinity County," Lester remembered. "He was thinkin' of buyin' this ranch. When he come back he says, 'Les if I buy that ranch, will you come up there and run it for me?"

A proven hand at any ranch chore, a high school graduate, footloose and free from a love interest and military service, Lester was the perfect candidate. Besides, why wouldn't Rega want to provide his grandson with a grand opportunity? And Lester, well, the idea appealed to him in a big way. He could see some new country, meet new people, be his own boss, and work toward being a huge success like his grandfather. Lester's enthusiasm consumed him. It was a chance of a lifetime; one that could set him up for life. With the gateway to triumph opening wide, Lester envisioned a most promising future.

Without hesitation Lester answered his grandfather's question and agreed to uproot. "I says, 'Yeah. I'll be glad to go up there', and Granddad said, 'Well, good, I'll see whether I really wanna buy that one or not'," Lester recalled.

Wow, a ranch with trees and an abundance of water; a place where grass grew tall and cattle got fat. Imagination was something that was never lacking with Lester. Though he'd never seen the Eel River, he pictured it as untamed as he was. At the prospect of change, Lester anticipated his grandfather's decision with a restlessness that was born of enthusiasm. Get excited? Lester? Oh, yeah. And why shouldn't he? Rega had Lester's best interests at heart. Always had, always would. Lester was certain of that above all else.

"Later, Granddad went back up and took my uncles with him to look at the ranch again. When he come home he was still thinkin' about buyin' it. That's when he had a stroke, a cerebral hemorrhage. He didn't last very long after that." Rega Dent Freeman died April 12, 1945, in Atascadero, California.

Suddenly the idea Rega had proposed to Lester, along with Lester's prospect of astonishing achievements, and his aspirations to prove himself to be as great of a man as he considered his grandfather to be - gone. The dream, the plan, the hopes no longer existed.

Worse yet was the grief Lester felt over his grandfather's absence. A disorienting sense of loss had occurred. Lester felt alone, adrift. A devoted and emotionally bonded relationship had ended too soon. Heartache was all that remained.

As he recalled the painful past, Lester readjusted his straw hat. He pushed it down lower on his forehead, then looked toward the ground and shook his head. "After my granddad passed away, I'd get on my horse and just ride out through the hills, not knowin' where I was goin'."

4 – DANCE WITH ME

"Kenny Branch, Bernice Burden and I had gone to a Grange dance in Parkfield one night," Lester began. "I played Cupid with Kenny and Bernice. I was the secret in-between person 'cause he was seein' someone else at the time."

BARBARA HATCH

Always on the lookout for fun and pretty women, that was the winter night Lester first spotted a young woman named Barbara Hatch across the hall.

DOLORES JONES, BARBARA HATCH, SILVIA HARLAN

"I saw this pretty gal and went over and asked her to dance," Lester said. "We had a drink out by my car that night." Lester and Barbara chatted, then went inside the Grange and danced some more. It was fun for the night but that was it.

A year went by before Lester saw Barbara for the second time at an Atascadero Grange installation of officers in 1946. Barbara, who was at that time, a Parkfield Grange member, was about to be inducted into the Pomona Grange. It was Lester's job, as the Marshall, to escort Barbara up to the podium. As he did, he couldn't help but ogle her as they marched along. She had eyes that spoke of self-confidence, a figure that graced the stage, a smile that warmed hearts, and a low cut dress that made Lester's eyes bulge and his heart pound.

"I said to myself, Holy Christ, I gotta have me some of that," Lester revealed. And the chase was on.

"I told my sister, Gladys, 'I'm gonna ask her for a date', and my sister says, 'You better not.' Well, I thought, to hell with you and took off and asked her. Then, when we started datin' my sister says, 'It won't last six months. You can't settle down, you're too damn crazy, wild'."

Lester and Barbara enjoyed each other's company over refreshments that night and despite his sister's dare of, 'you better not' - or maybe, in part, because of it, Lester wasted no time securing a date to see Barbara again.

Their first date was the following weekend. Lester drove east into Kern County to Annette, near Annette's Civil Defense Observation Station, where Barbara had volunteered during the war. Several miles south of Cholame he picked up Barbara to go to a dance. Over Highway 46 and back up Highway 101 into Monterey County, Lester and Barbara went to the Hames Valley Grange. The hall was tucked up against the foothills of the Santa Lucia Mountains. It was a beautiful setting, a brisk and starry evening - one that lent itself to country boy style romance.

Outside the dance, twenty year old Lester leaned into Barbara for his first kiss, ever. It was the beginning of something special and Lester knew it. A few more kisses and soon his eagerness got the better of him. He reached out.

"I tried to feel her up but she said 'I'm not that kind of girl'," Lester confessed, then laughed. It was January 12, 1946, Barbara's twenty-first birthday.

In his 1939 Plymouth coup, Lester's first car, he sped around the curvy country roads for sixty miles to pick up Barbara for their regular Saturday night dates. Every weekend they drove another untold number of miles to go to a dance, even as far away as the Carrisa Plains.

LESTER ROUGEOT AND BARBARA HATCH
ON A DATE AT THE MORRO BAY RODEO

It didn't take long for Lester's affection to grow to a feverish level. To wait for the weekend to be with Barbara just wouldn't do. There was a sense of urgency about his need to be with her as often as possible. Before long, during the week, as well as the weekends, he found himself driving the one hundred twenty mile round trip repeatedly. Lester couldn't get enough of Barbara. Her competent character and confident personality kept him on his toes. Her amiable girl-next-door smile, her kind, yet adventurous eyes, her lovely face, and admittedly her cleavage, captivated Lester.

Barbara's straightforward – few words need to be spoken - Dutch nature also attracted Lester. She was like no one he had ever met. He had a challenge on his hands and he liked it. By that point Lester was in hot pursuit. Whatever it took to make Barbara his, he was willing.

As his way to romance Barbara was not by showering her with impractical gifts, Lester decided he would purchase hats for Barbara and himself. "Stetsons back then were better quality. I wanted her and I to have matching hats, so the hats were the same make and color. The only difference was," Lester admitted, "I pinched mine so I'd look taller."

LESTER AND BARBARA - MATCHING HATS

During their daytime dates, Lester took Barbara fishing, squirrel hunting, or just driving around so they could be together. Once accompanied by Lester's younger sister, Mildred "Sis" and her date, Donald "Donkey" or "Bud" Barba, the couple enjoyed taking in scenery, stopping for an occasional cigarette, having a drink, and cruising the country.

"Bud's the one who drove the Dadar's egg truck up Indian Valley," Lester informed. "Sis didn't marry him."

MILDRED "SIS" ROUGEOT AND DONALD BARBA

On one particular fishing outing, Barbara decided she wanted to get to the other side of the river. Rather than have her remove her shoes, roll up her Levi pant legs, and wade across the water, Lester, ever so gallantly, whisked her off the ground into his strong arms to carry her through the raging currents. Okay, so it was the Salinas River near Bradley, and it was rippling not raging. Nevertheless, for a moment it was chivalry in action, the fearless and heroic young cowboy lifting the maiden into his arms to carry her across the mighty river.

The scenario tickled Lester's funny bone. He began to laugh. So hard, in fact, that – oops - he dropped his love right in the middle of the river. Splash. There in the water was a fully clothed Barbara thrashing around trying to stand up. And, lucky for Lester, she was laughing. Barbara not only took her soaking in stride she thought it was humorous. What a gal.

Approximately two months after their first date, in March of 1946, Lester had taken Barbara to a dance in either San Ardo or Hames Valley where, he confessed, "We'd had a little too much to drink."

DONALD BARBA AND LESTER ROUGEOT

After the dance they, along with friend, Francis McKanna, pulled an 'almost-all-nighter' at Francis' house in Bradley. And although Lester and Barbara did manage to nod off and catch a few winks on the couch that night, they were up bright and early the following morning. Together they took a drive along Big Sandy Creek up Indian Valley.

Still in their clothes from the night before and armed with their .22 caliber rifles, Lester drove into the most remote area of the valley. A hidden and secret world, the terrain was far from unfamiliar to Lester. It was there that he had built roads with his father and honed his hunting and horsemanship skills. Not only was the area much more than part of Lester's stomping grounds, the far reaches of the valleys that he knew so well, the place he had demonstrated his masculine prowess time and time again, had also been his private proving grounds.

LESTER ROUGEOT AND BARBARA HATCH

Once they arrived at the mouth of Buzzard Canyon which - as a crow flies in a slight arch - is about half way between San Miguel and Coalinga, there in the middle of no man's land, Lester stopped the car.

No words were spoken as he and Barbara crossed the creek with their rifles, then sat down on the other side. Nothing but the sounds and sights of nature surrounded them as they dug their heels in the dirt.

Then Barbara broke the silence. "Do you remember what you asked me last night?"

Lester looked over at Barbara. "Yeah, I remember," he said.

Barbara hadn't been sure she could take Lester seriously the night before. She had opted to decline answering his question but wasn't willing to wait any longer to address it. So there she sat on the creek bank, still and quiet as she waited for Lester to take charge of the situation. She stared into his blue eyes.

"I asked you to marry me," Lester blurted. "You gonna marry me, or not?"

BARBARA HATCH AND LESTER ROUGEOT

"Yeah," Barbara said with a smile. "I'll marry you."

Sealed with a kiss, the couple agreed they would marry - the sooner the better as far as Lester was concerned. At that point he had decided to buy Barbara an engagement ring. He went to the jeweler on Twelfth Street, who happened to be Barbara's uncle, Jim Colyer. When asked if Barbara had accompanied him to pick out the ring, Lester confided, "No. I was afraid she might like one I couldn't afford." He chose the ring himself and would give it to Barbara the following day.

LESTER ROUGEOT AND BARBARA HATCH
IN HARE CANYON

"I was a fast worker," Lester boasted. Without any fanfare, Lester dug into his pocket, pulled out the engagement ring, and put it on Barbara's finger. If it hadn't been official before, it was then. From their first date to the altar it was a few days shy of four months.

"My sister, Gladys," Lester disclosed, "thought we had to get married."

In a sense, Lester did have to marry Barbara, not because she was already pregnant but because as Lester revealed with a laugh, "She wouldn't give me any so I had to marry her."

About to be married on the ninth of April in 1946, at the old Paso Robles Baptist Church on Park Street, the twenty year old groom put on his one and only suit, the same one his parents had purchased for him to wear to the Paso Robles High School prom. Heart full of happiness Lester stood at the altar and waited for the organist, Ada Hendricks, to play the first notes of the wedding march. Lester watched Barbara walk down the aisle with her father, Everett Hatch. Everett gave his daughter's hand in marriage and Reverend Paul Brown then performed the ceremony.

LESTER AND BARBARA ROUGEOT
APRIL 9, 1946

Feeling both pride and pleasure Lester recited his vows. His best man, Uncle R.D. 'Babe' Freeman, stood to his side. Lester's bride stood with her matron of honor, her sister, Alice Miller. Lester's cousin, Richard Freeman was the ring bearer and cousin, Judy Freeman was the flower girl.

R.D."BABE" FREEMAN – BEST MAN,
RICHARD FREEMAN – RING BEARER
LESTER AND BARBARA ROUGEOT – GROOM AND BRIDE
ALICE MILLER – MATRON OF HONOR
JUDY FREEMAN – FLOWER GIRL

A reception followed at the church after which the newlyweds would spend their first night as husband and wife at Maryanna's, a motel at the corner of Eighth and Spring Streets in Paso Robles. "We didn't have any dancing at our wedding reception." Lester's eyes twinkled. "We did our dancin' in the motel," he said with a smile and a sigh, "Room ten. I'll never forget that night."

The next day the newlyweds drove up to King City where they got a room near a concert hall. Dinner that night was paid for by

Shorty Williams, a cattle buyer and friend who happened to be in the restaurant that night and wanted to congratulate the newlyweds. Breakfast the next morning was a wedding gift from Tommy Duncan. Tommy was a Western swing vocalist, pianist, and songwriter for the band Lester and Barbara had seen the night before, Bob Wills and the Texas Playboys. Lester and Barbara were thrilled.

After their morning meal, no doubt singing songs from the night before, such as the one that comes to Lester's mind first, San Antonio Rose, he and Barbara headed for the coast. At Pacific Grove they decided to take a tour of 17-mile drive to Pebble Beach. The scenic road wound around the Monterey Peninsula past the well-known trademark for the area, a lone cypress tree growing on a rock near the water's edge. Along the coastline and through the Del Monte Forest the newlyweds enjoyed the views, some of which had been captured on film in 1944 just two years previously in the movie National Velvet starring Elizabeth Taylor and Mickey Rooney.

South of Pebble Beach the couple continued to drive down the Pacific Coast Highway One. The narrow southbound lane of the highway gave Barbara, the passenger, the most dramatic front row seat from which to view the rugged coastline and the crashing waves below. The Bluebird Motel in Cambria was the final night of their honeymoon after which they drove down to San Luis Obispo, to see Grandpa and Grandma Rougeot and then drove home up Highway 101.

Though the honeymoon had come to an end - the fun and adventure's had just begun.

5 – CARRIAGES AND COTTON

Upon returning from their honeymoon, newlyweds, Mr. and Mrs. Lester Rougeot made themselves at home in Lester's room at his family's ranch in Indian Valley. They lived with Lester's parents for about two months and according to Lester, Barbara got along very well with Clarence and Thelma. Their new daughter-in-law pitched in where she could, helping with both housework and farm work.

"She even mowed hay," Lester boasted.

That summer Lester worked for his uncle, Babe Freeman, and the couple moved in with his grandmother, Dovie Freeman for a short time.

"Grandpa had already passed away by then, the year before. The same year Roosevelt died. That was hard," Lester said. "I was real attached to him. I spent a lot of time with him."

When harvest work started for Pete Mulhall, Lester and Barbara found a duplex to rent in Paso Robles.

Later that year, in December of 1946, the couple moved again when they bought a home together.

"This guy by the name of Whitley had started a housing project in 1927," Lester told. "But we bought our house in Whitley Gardens from Slim Thomas. He was a cowboy up at the San Marcos Ranch."

Marriage and nesting didn't stop the newlyweds from going out and having fun. They continued to enjoy a social life, dancing, pranking, family obligations, and work. The happily married couple also managed some alone time. At six months into their life as husband and wife, Barbara conceived. The couple was elated as

Barbara blossomed. Far from staying at home, living on the couch, watching television soap operas, Barbara not only kept pace with her active husband - as well as the men he worked with - she sometimes outshined them. Pregnancy didn't slow her down in the least.

"If I needed help doin' somethin'," Lester said, "Barb was right there to help me. She knew everything about the ranch. She knew more than the men did."

It was at the Hillman Place, on Estrella Road across Highway 46 from Lester and Barbara's home in River Grove/Whitley Gardens. Lester did everything for his employer, Pete Mulhall, from carpentry to cowboy chores.

"I was horseback one day, near the reservoir out next to the barn I built for Homer Hillman," Lester told. "I had roped this calf and one of the guys I worked for had come in the corral to help me mark it."

With its head tethered to Lester's rope the calf jumped around like a trout hooked to a fishing line. This made it difficult for the one-man ground crew.

"He ran after that calf and tried to catch it by the hind feet," Lester explained. "That guy couldn't catch nothin'." Around and around they went but the calf managed to evade capture.

That's when Barbara, who was nearing her due date with Regina, stepped in. She marched over to the man.

"Barb grabbed the rope out of his hand, then caught the calf by both heels," Lester marveled. "I'll never forget that."

Amazed at his very pregnant powerhouse wife, Lester then took the rope from Barbara, marked the calf, and the task was accomplished.

"Those are the things we did all of our lives," Lester recalled. "Helpin' each other." The love and respect in Lester's eyes was obvious as he spoke of Barbara.

"We did all kinds of things together. I got the credit but Barb was always part of what I did."

By all accounts, marriage suited Lester. The physical closeness, the emotional ties, the familial connections, and most of all, the bond with his wife, were what mattered most. The security and the acceptance that Barbara brought into Lester's life agreed with him. Lester thrived in his wife's company. What was to come was made possible by the woman who stood beside him and the children with whom they were about to be blessed.

As Lester said, and continues to say so many times, he couldn't have chosen anyone better for himself. Barbara was pretty, she was fun, and she was game for most anything. From the start their marriage had the potential to be a successful, productive, never-a-dull-moment partnership.

Fifteen months after their wedding bells chimed, it was time to buy a baby carriage. At two weeks shy of twenty-two years old, Lester became a father for the first time. On July 4, 1947, along came Regina Francis Rougeot. Baby Regina was named after Lester's influential and favorite grandfather on his mother's side, Rega Freeman.

"Regina got more attention than any baby ever born," Lester said with an amused expression on his face. "Even the neighbor ladies would come over to play with her."

FIRST TIME FATHER
LESTER ROUGEOT WITH BABY CARRIAGE - 1947

LESTER ROUGEOT HOLDS DAUGHTER REGINA
DARLENE CRASPAY LOOKS ON

One year and two days after Regina was born, on July 6, 1948, out came Chester Clarence Rougeot, named after Lester's twin brother and also his father. Margie Annette Rougeot was born two years later on June 25, 1950. Her middle name is the same as Barbara's hometown.

Lester recalled with a laugh, "Barb used to say, 'You just throw your pants on the bed and I get pregnant'."

Though they had a house full of children, Lester still liked to flirt with his wife. "One time I called the house and changed my voice all romantic," Lester told. "I was sayin' stuff like, Hey, there good lookin'. How 'bout a date? About half hour later I showed up at the house and found her all dolled up."

Lester laughed as he recalled his relationship with the mother of his children.

"There was nothin' she wouldn't do for me," Lester asserted.

LESTER ROUGEOT – 1948

LESTER ROUGEOT AT WORK - 1948
MOVING BRUSH, INDIAN VALLEY

LESTER AND CHESTER ROUGEOT

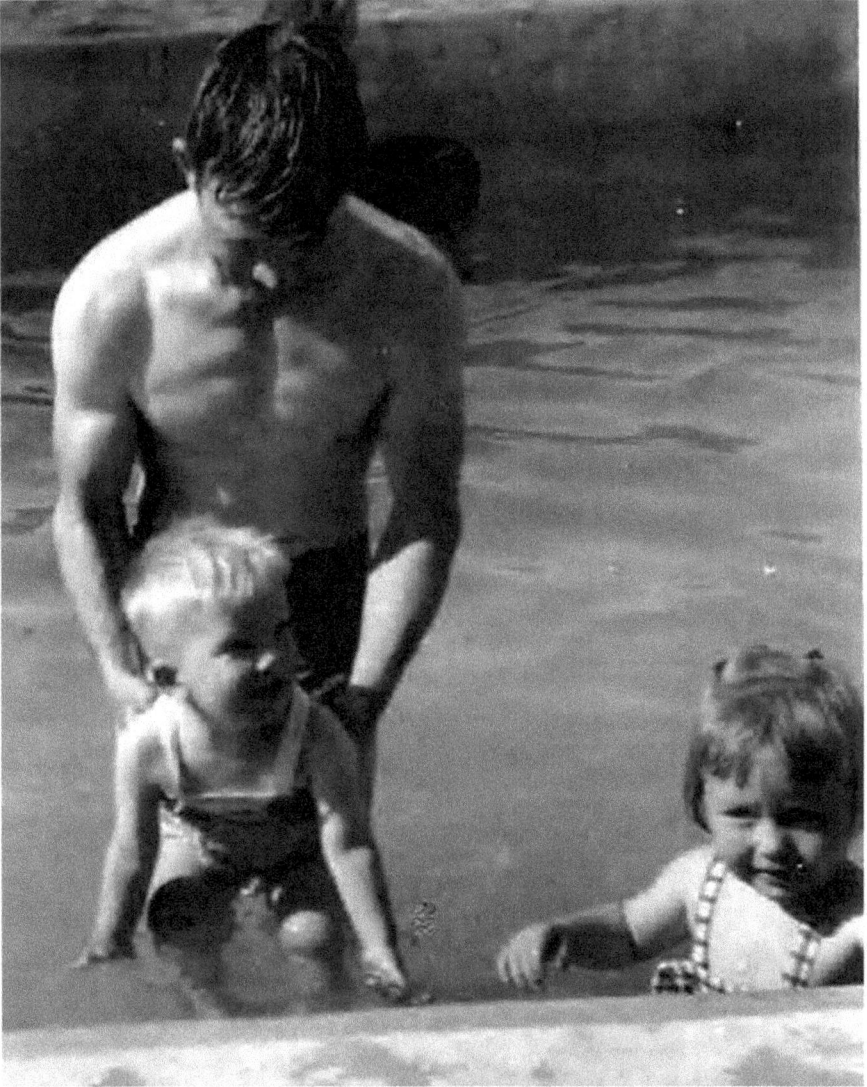

LESTER ROUGEOT WITH CHESTER AND REGINA
SHANDON POOL

Having small children didn't mean Lester and Barbara neglected their outdoor activities. From the start, the Rougeot children were conditioned to take part in everything from harvests to hunting.

"When Chester was small, Lester accidently killed a spike," Lester's cousin, Ken Freeman revealed. "Of course he didn't want anyone to know about it but the word spread rapidly. Lester and

Chester were in town after that and someone, maybe Charlie Schinbine, was in the group and got Chester to talking. Then he asked if they had killed a buck."

Young Chester blurted out an honest answer.

"Of course Chester said, 'Yes, daddy got a buck'. How many horns did it have? Chester threw up both hands with one finger on each hand. 'These many,' he exclaimed," Ken Freeman told. "All had a great laugh."

Even though Lester worked long days, whenever he was home, and the children were awake, he was a hands on dad, one who seemed to have a knack for activating smiles, giggles, and silliness. Lester was the kind of dad who often joined his children on the ground or the floor to interact face to face.

CHRISTMAS - 1948
AT THE INDIAN VALLEY ROUGEOT RANCH

Holidays were all about family. Christmas Eve was always with Lester's parents, Clarence and Thelma, at their Indian Valley Ranch. Christmas Day Lester and Barbara took their children to Barbara's sister and her husband's house, Alice and Raymond Miller, in Parkfield. On many occasions when the family got together to celebrate, the photographers always seemed to catch Lester down at kid level.

LESTER ROUGEOT
NAP TIME AFTER SHOOTING OAK BALLS OUT OF A TREE

In their early months of marriage, Lester earned a living by working several different jobs, just several weeks, here and there. But that was about to change.

"I was in town one day when Morrie Wildman's secretary spotted me," Lester said. "She went back to work and told Wildman if he wanted to talk with me he could find me up town."

When Morrie Wildman caught up with Lester he had a proposal. He needed to hire a competent manager for his family's cotton and alfalfa farm in the Bakersfield area, someone he could trust. He thought of Lester. Why Lester? Well, when a person comes along who tolerates toil, tackles whatever predicament pops up, and does it in good cheer – that's a guy that's in high demand. And that's Lester. Wildman saw it. He sought out Lester and made his pitch.

Lester went home and discussed the idea with Barbara. Although the couple had recently purchased their house in River Grove/Whitley Gardens, and had three small children to consider, they accepted Wildman's job offer, which required them to move. They rented out their house, packed the car, and off they drove toward the unknown.

"I'd never seen cotton before," Lester admitted. Though he was inexperienced with the crops he was about to tend, Lester was no greenhorn farmer. At twenty-five years old Lester had twenty-five years of farm experience under his belt. Where he'd come from was hillsides of dry farmed grains that could be harvested with mechanical equipment. Where he was destined for was a farm where crops required irrigation, some of which involved a labor intensive harvest by hired hands.

"I went to work for Morrie Wildman in 1951. He sent me to his mother's cotton ranch East of Bakersfield out by Weedpatch and Arvin. I'd never farmed cotton but I learnt real fast," Lester recalled. "Barb and our three small children, Regina, Chester and Margie moved the hundred miles with me. It was a good decision."

As with everything else in life, Lester and Barbara turned the job into family activities and adventure. While farming one hundred twenty acres of cotton and forty acres of alfalfa, Barbara was often operator of a tractor. When an extra hand was needed it wasn't unusual to put a wife, or even a child, behind the wheel of a farm vehicle. Lester's first born, daughter Regina, remembers her dad teaching her how to drive one day when he needed someone to steer an old door-less, seat-less Dodge pickup around the fields.

There on a wooden box meant to be a seat, Regina sat with her feet dangling as she took control of the wheel.

"I was about four years old and we were living on a cotton ranch east of Bakersfield that Dad was managing," Regina began. "He needed help putting irrigation octopuses out and Mom couldn't help because of taking care of a small baby and another small child, so he took me with him."

REGINA ROUGEOT, HARRY MILLER, DOUG THOMASON,
MARGIE ROUGEOT, CHESTER ROUGEOT

Regina described an irrigation octopus as a round cylinder about three or four feet high with round holes around the sides where six to eight feet long rubber tubes were inserted. A supply of octopuses had been stacked in the back of the door-less Dodge.

"The round cylinder fit over the irrigation valve where water came out and then out the arms to the different rows so you could water several rows at the same time. Dad sat me on the box, started the pickup, put it in low, and told me to steer the pickup to the end of the row while he walked beside the pickup putting out the octopuses."

No doubt about it, farming was a family affair for the Rougeot's. What Lester's trust in his daughter did for her was to demonstrate he believed in her capabilities. It served to build her confidence and as Regina said, "It made me feel like a big girl."

THE ROUGEOT CHILDREN

Not only did Lester and Barbara's children learn how essential it was to lend a cooperative and helping hand, they learned responsibility, and were instilled with what today is becoming an uncommon work ethic. Best of all, the Rougeot children grew up experiencing the true meaning of family. Just as Lester and Barbara had been born into families that embraced them, so too had Regina, Chester, and Margie.

Although the young family had moved one hundred miles away from the Paso Robles area they made it a priority to secure the ties that bound the extended family. Fishing and hunting outings were favored times of togetherness for those adventurous family members who loved the great outdoors.

MARGIE, REGINA, CHESTER, AND LESTER ROUGEOT – 1952

CLARENCE AND THELMA ROUGEOT
THIRTIETH ANNIVERSARY 1952

In anticipation of a group fishing trip the following day, to the Sierras, the Rougeot's Bakersfield house was full of people. As unpredictable situations often occur on working farms and ranches, there are times plans have to be put aside and everything has to be dropped so as to attend to the most urgent task at hand. Anything to do with water, accidents, and livestock emergencies generally go straight to the top of the list of priorities. But in California, not only are there every day normal common catastrophes, there's this near constant threat of unexpected tremors and terror that shakes up life and tears apart the land.

"We were in Bakersfield when the Tehachapi earthquake hit in 1952," Lester says. "When the shakin' started early that mornin', Barb went out the bedroom window to the front porch where Regina and John and Margaret Kalar's daughter, Dovie, were sleeping. John and Margaret had come over from Taft with their kids. They were asleep in the living room on the fold out couch in front of the fire place. They were worried about the fireplace fallin' on 'em. Margaret was runnin' around with just a sheet wrapped around 'er. Little did they realize a big deer head hung over the couch. Their boys, Bill and David, and Chester were asleep at the other end of the porch. Margie was asleep in her crib in our room. We all gathered on the porch to watch in amazement at the transformers goin' off all over the valley. We watched as a black man who was changin' irrigation water pulled up in the front of the house. He got out of the car not realizin' what was goin' on. The ground started shakin' and rollin'. It must have taken him a good five minutes to get back in his car, but when he did, all you saw were the taillights goin' high speed down the dusty road."

"Everyone went to the Sierras as planned and Dad stayed behind to make sure everything was taken care at the cotton ranch, helping his neighbors who didn't have water," Lester's daughter Regina said. "He was the only one in the area who had water because of the type of pump he had."

"I farmed eighteen hours a day," Lester stated. "Barb raised the kids and she did upholstery, too, furniture and tractor seats." Although Lester was out the door before his children woke up and back in the door for the night after they had gone to bed he said, "We always had dinner together at six o'clock."

Family meal times were a chance for Lester and Barbara to serve as role models, promote healthy eating habits, and establish family traditions. It was important to both parents that they encourage family unity as well. Dinners, and those days they all worked together, served as rich soil in which to grow deep roots that would secure the Rougeot family and contribute to their devotion for one another.

DOVIE FREEMAN WITH HER GREAT GRANDCHILDREN
REGINA ROUGEOT - SECOND FROM LEFT, CHESTER – THIRD,
MARGIE - FOURTH

"One day, Margie was on Barb's lap with Regina and Chester sittin' on the back of the trailer," Lester recalled. "I was stackin' hay bales as they came off the hay loader."

With good humor Lester recounted the day his wife drove the tractor and veered off course.

"There were a bunch of bee boxes set up by the side of the field." Lester hollered to caution Barbara.

The childhood fear and trauma he had suffered near the honey bee tree, with his twin brother Chester, came to mind. Lester motioned wildly with his arms to keep Barbara from getting too close. The last thing he wanted was the noise and vibrations from the tractor to disturb the bees.

Somewhat like all the bells and whistles at a railroad crossing, Lester's voice and phobic display of body language advised of impending danger. The thought of having to flee another swarm of angry bees, and at the same time having to save his family from an air force of tiny suicide soldiers, well, it was menacing.

"I don't like those little yellow and black flying bombs," Lester explained. "I yelled at Barb to head the other way."

When she finally turned around and looked at Lester, he caught a glimpse of Barbara's expression. That's when the switch in his head was flipped and the light went on. He realized his beloved wife, the mother of his adored children, had steered the tractor toward the bees, on purpose.

Barbara glanced back again.

"She was laughin' like crazy," Lester laughed.

Finally Barbara empathized with her energetic and wide-eyed husband. She turned the tractor back to the hay bales and back to work without incident.

Relieved, Lester looked at his first and second born children, "I turned around and Reg and Chester were gettin' a kick out of seein' another prank their mom had pulled on their dad. Guess she decided to liven things up a little out in the hay field."

Hmm, sounds familiar. And why shouldn't Barbara pull practical jokes on her husband? Married to a man who was full of surprises, she never knew *what* was next, though she knew *something* was bound to happen. Even something as straightforward as going to a quiet bar for a cocktail could turn into an outrageous evening with Lester dancing by himself – up on a table.

Although Barbara was known to pull a good prank on Lester, now and then, she was also known as an organized and authoritative woman, who kept the family of five from being in constant chaos.

"Dad was not the disciplinarian," daughter, Regina revealed. "That was Mom's job."

"Barb did a great job with the kids," Lester credited. "She did everything with them. Took 'em to all their activities."

"That's why we're so stable," son Chester said and chuckled.

"Yeah, she kept the kids stable," Lester agreed as he threw his head back in laughter. "I'd of had 'em in trouble."

That's believable.

"When we lived in Bakersfield, Dad befriended a man who was a highway patrolman," Chester recalled. "They enjoyed pullin' pranks on one another." Chester, remembered a market at an intersection, owned by yet another friend, where locals would meet for coffee and conversation.

"One day the patrolman was there havin' coffee when Dad snuck out for awhile."

What was Lester doing while his patrolman friend was inside enjoying a break at the local hangout? Nothing - according to Lester.

"It was the judge's secretary," he claimed. Next to the store there was a building where Judge Parrish held General District court and somehow his young legal assistant got an idea. All on her own she formulated this plan. Yeah, right. Anyone who knows Lester, knows it's not a stretch to imagine he egged on and dared his secretary friend, at the very least.

"Cattaneo was her name," Lester recalled.

The mischief makers stood outside the store as if they were innocent bystanders and watched as the highway patrolman pulled away from the market. He'd go a few feet and stop. Try again and stop. He got out of his black and white patrol car, looked all around and under it, but couldn't locate the source of a loud metallic rattle. Though he failed to find the problem, he was sure there was one. He called for a tow truck.

"The mechanic at the shop about tore that car up tryin' to find what was wrong with it," Lester roared. Come to find out, the terrible racket the car made when it moved, came from the wheels. Turned out the judge's secretary knew right where she could find a tire iron to pop open the patrol car's hubcaps and put rocks inside. Not something most women would think to do but, that's Lester's story and he's stickin' to it.

Later Lester revealed, "This gal, the judge's secretary, she was a beautiful girl, she always wanted me to go horseback ridin' with her but I never did. I knew what was gonna happen, I'd get in trouble. I never did go out with anybody when we was married."

Smart man. Though Lester was into stirring things up, he knew better than to betray his wife, a woman nicknamed "Dead eye Barb".

"One time when I went up there to the store, Johnny's store," Lester began, "there was this one guy, Billy Lundquist, he came with his Chevy car that he pulled his cotton trailer with." Lester couldn't help himself from throwing the proverbial monkey wrench in this man's day. Known for his annoying habit of borrowing everyone's tools and equipment, rather than buying his own, the man was a bit of a rub for Lester.

"We used to pick on 'im 'cause he was kinda cheap. When he went inside the store I reached down and pulled the pin out of his trailer hitch. He didn't have a safety chain. When he got in his car to drive away he got all the way home before he realized there was no trailer." Lester laughed. Yep, opportunity presented itself and Lester seized it - no big news there. What did become big news around the cotton mill was what happened when Billy finally bought some tools.

"He had a three quarter inch drive socket set he bought, so I stole 'em outta his car and threw 'em into his cotton trailer. Well, when it went thru the gin, the guys in there found it. The people in front of the gin had it in the office and *I* didn't even know where it was. Then this one guy, Eddie Yackovich, he was in on it with me, so when he found out the tools had disappeared he thought we was gonna have to buy another set of tools. Oh, he was excited as hell. He was another cheapy. The gals in the office was laughin' like hell. They finally confessed where the tools were and gave 'em back."

No doubt about it, people who seek and enjoy life's pleasures – humor being one of the greatest – runs in Lester's family. Lester had good teachers in his dad and his grandfather Freeman. Lester's children were also taught by a master good-time guy.

Lester's son Chester maintained himself to be, "a straight arrow" and would never think to be the cause of excitement.

To his son's "straight-arrow" claim, Lester said, "BS." Lester knew his son, Chester, had studied the fine art of prank pulling and took part from a young age. In fact, Chester enjoyed it when his dad played tricks on people, especially, when he got to participate.

Like the day they were at the Bakersfield farm and Lester had hired a man to cultivate cotton. When the man was working in the field, and while Lester's impressionable son observed, and learned how it was done, Lester jacked up the man's pickup and put a block under the axle. Why? Just for fun. To cause some excitement.

When the man was done working for the day, he got in his pickup to leave. By then Chester, not wanting to miss the show, had perched himself on a wood pile. There he sat. He waited and watched. Lester, on the other hand, was nowhere to be seen by that time.

The man turned on the ignition, shifted into reverse, and gave it the gas. The engine raced, but the pickup remained stationary. He shifted into drive. Same thing happened. This delighted young Chester, who sat on the wood, and laughed.

When the man finally figured out what the problem was he asked Chester, "Did Shorty do this?"

"Nope," Chester said with a hint of glee and pride in his reply as he confessed, "Me and my dad did."

There were many interesting employees hired over the years when Lester was in charge of the Wildman's Bakersfield farm. They seemed to come from all walks of life. Several of them were most memorable because of their peculiarities. But no matter how unusual someone else might have perceived a few of these characters, Lester proved time and time again to be an equal opportunity employer before such a thing was popular protocol and put into law.

"When Dad went to Bakersfield, he knew nothing of cotton farming," Lester's daughter, Regina began. "An old Mexican named Hombrea helped Dad learn how to irrigate the cotton fields. Now Hombrea understood no English and Dad understood no Spanish. Mom understood a little Spanish but was not always available to translate. So, Dad and Hombrea devised their own way of communicating. They drew pictures in the dirt. Hombrea must have been seventy years old, about Dad's size in stature, and these two grown men each with a stick in hand, drawing pictures in the dirt in the middle of a road was quite a sight. It worked and mission was accomplished."

Hired to handpick the cotton and paid by the pound there was one woman who always came to work with her dog. The woman's little sidekick, just a pint-sized pooch, trailed her up and down the rows.

"That little thing followed her all day, every day," Lester said. "It was her constant companion."

No one thought much of it until they discovered why the woman's daily yields were so impressive. In each bag that was weighed at the scales, the woman managed to slip that little bit of canine in with her cotton.

Then there was the man who packed around a jug of wine with him at work. Rochester the Wino, he called himself and even had Lester make his paychecks out to that name. Rochester the Wino would toss the bottle up the row then work his way toward it. He'd take a drink and toss the bottle up the row a ways further and so on and so forth. Not so unusual perhaps. What was odd – as he picked cotton, he had an ongoing conversation with *his* constant companion - the jug.

Of the workers he had employed Lester remembered a crew of black women he hired to weed and thin the cotton crop.

"I'd cultivate up to 'em then chop with 'em. They worked for less and were the hardest workin' bunch," Lester praised. "And funny too. I'll never forget this one gal. She was talkin' about a man she knew and she says, 'Do you know it cost two hundred and fifty dollars to bury him? He wasn't worth two hundred fifty dollars!'

In more of a statement than a complaint the woman made mention of the working conditions and how they affected her.

Lester took on an accent as he belly laughed and told, "She said, 'These gall darn bugs in my brassiere are about to drive me crazy', it was so funny the way she said it."

Not only did Lester hire help to work in the fields, he sometimes found people in the cotton who weren't working.

"When the kids were with me one night checkin' irrigation I caught a couple in my spotlight," Lester told while he laughed. Evidently Lester's cotton fields were considered a lover's lane of sorts. "When the light hit 'em the kids asked me what those people were doin' in there and I told 'em, 'Oh, they're just checkin' the cotton'."

The last two years the young Rougeot family lived and worked on the Wildman's cotton farm near Bakersfield, Lester used a mechanical cotton picker. After the harvest, what remained of the cotton plants were left to dry in the field, then chopped. Lester hired an extra man to do the chopping with him.

When the hired man noticed Lester shoot a rabbit one day he asked, "What do ya do with them rabbits?"

Rabbits were considered destructive to the crops. As with ground squirrels, the normal practice was for farmers to shoot them on sight and leave them for nature's cleanup crew, the buzzards. When the hired man learned the rabbits were going to waste, he jumped at the opportunity to bring them home for his family to eat.

With Lester's permission, the man was allowed to shoot Jack rabbits in the fields, store them in the irrigation pots to keep them cool, until he got off work, and take them home.

But rabbit hunting wasn't just for the men. Barbara was known to take the shotgun Lester had given her and shoot rabbits as well.

DEAD EYE BARB

"Parker Brothers manufactured a great shotgun but they have one problem," Lester's son, Chester said. "They're light weight so they tend to have high recoil. They kick like a mule. I was buggin' Mom to let me shoot a Jack rabbit for awhile. She finally said, 'okay', just to shut me up. I could just get it to my shoulder and hold it steady."

When a Jack rabbit ran out, Chester pulled the trigger of his mother's double barreled sixteen gauge shotgun. Pow! He was propelled backwards.

"Flat on my back," Chester said and laughed. "It was years before I asked Mom to let me shoot her shotgun again."

At the time the gun seemed heavy to Chester, but later when he began to use it for quail and dove hunting and he discovered that wasn't true.

"It still had a kick to it," Chester added.

* * *

CHESTER, REGINA, AND MARGIE ROUGEOT
WITH THEIR COUSIN HARRY MILLER

During those years near Bakersfield in the Weedpatch and Arvin area, Lester belonged to an organization that sponsored a father/son night.

"For entertainment they had some can-can dancers," Lester's son, Chester said disclosed, "The dancers were actually men from the organization. Dad was a very perty dancer. Us kids had a great time watchin' Mom make 'im up for his performance."

"Chester was on the bed in the bedroom watching Mom dress dad," Regina added, "and got to laughing so hard he fell off the bed."

CHESTER, MARGIE, AND REGINA ROUGEOT

Ever the civic minded individual, Lester also participated in the Lamont Rodeo as their chairman and was the barn foreman for the fair in Bakersfield. As his parents and grandparents had mentored him to do, he took it upon himself to care for his family *and* his community.

Those early years of their marriage were demanding. It was a life full of labor, love, and laughter. Not an hour of their hectic days went by when the couple wasn't tending to something.

Lester marveled at how active they were back then and said, "I don't know how we ever did all the things we did."

Would all the farm duties, household tasks, community activities, and daily family responsibilities mellow Lester, mature him and keep him from being such a jokester?

Not even close.

CHESTER, REGINA, AND MARGIE ROUGEOT
WITH RUDY THE DOG

6 – THE INTERNATIONAL MAN

Wheat and barley, four thousand acres of it, on a ranch that could get, as Lester said, "Hotter than hell", that was the Keyes Valley Ranch, one of Lester's next projects. That, along with two thousand acres, of equally as sweltering grain fields, on the nearby Hillman land, was where Lester took on everything from harvesting to farm equipment repair.

No more cotton for Lester. In the fall of 1955, he and his young family moved back to their house just east of Paso Robles and it was Whitley Gardens for good. Though he would continue to work for Morrie Wildman, Lester was back at home where he knew the land and the people intimately as well as all the good hunting spots.

Hunting and family seemed to go hand in hand with the Rougeots and their relatives. It was a way the family stayed bonded, a reason to celebrate and feast together. Sometimes they'd go out, find food, bag it, and tag it. Other times it was more of a shoot it, cook it, and consume it day.

The first weekend of dove hunting was always a big family event. Everyone gathered at Barbara's parent's property, the Everett Hatch Ranch in the Annette area near the San Luis Obispo and Kern County lines.

"The Ken Araujo family, Helen Hatch (Graces's and sister), Dad and Mom and family, Raymond and Alice Miller, and Harry and Jessie Wolf aka"Dommie", Helen and Grace's mother, gathered early in the morning," Regina said. "Fay Araujo, Grace, Helen, and Dommie would stay at the house with the youngest children while the rest of the crew went out and took positions around the ranch south of the shop. They would wait for the doves to come for food and water."

It was a strategy that served them well.

Lester's daughter Regina remembered, "Kids too old to stay home with the youngest but not old enough to shoot a shotgun, were assigned the job of bird dogs."

Shooters downed the birds, the children retrieved them. Much easier to train than dogs. The downside of the dog versus human bird dog issue – children wised up unlike dogs that would fetch for years and never once complain about it.

"Gracie and the other women would have the noon day meal ready when the hunters came back in to clean their kill," Regina said. "I remember Gracie having a big dish pan to put the cleaned birds in and then would take and put them under the bed in the back of the house in case the game warden came by to check the limits taken during the morning hunt."

That must have been one of those shoot, swallow, and shut up days. Yum, yum. All gone. Finger-lickin' good. Nothin' but a few bones, a pile of feathers, and some of the innards to dispose of and it's, 'Doves? What doves?'

"In the territory surrounding the town of Annette, near Cholame, the first day of dove season every year, we'd go," Chester began. "We'd shoot doves in the morning, pick 'em and get 'em all clean and put 'em in a big porcelain tub and then we'd hide 'em under the bed in case the game warden came then we'd go back in the afternoon and shoot 'em again.

"Down there where Takken's is now, that used to be a mom and pop grocery store owned by Ken Araujo. Sometimes he and his wife and boys would come out, he had a .410. That's what he shot doves with a .410. And his son had a side by side .410."

Chester's head tipped back and he laughed. "Grandpa Hatch would not eat anything that had feathers."

"Yeah, Everett Hatch, Barb's dad, he wouldn't eat nothin' that had feathers on it," Lester agreed. "We'd come back from Parkfield, went back up there and spent the night at Barb's folks and the next morning Frank Hatch, her brother, came out with his father-in-law and he wanted me to go chukar huntin' with 'em. I says, 'Ah baloney. You ain't gonna kill no chukars. They can take off and fly a long way.

"So we went chukar huntin' and I killed one. And then I found out how to kill those chukars. When they fly off into this other canyon you wait about an hour or so, on the point where they fly over, and they come back."

"This one time on one of Dommie's last visits to the ranch, Gracie had baked an apple pie," Regina recalled. "When mother Dommie cut into daughter Gracie's pie, she commented that the pie wasn't done. This gave the group the perfect thing to rib Gracie over for years to come. A family favorite she didn't get teased about, was the shrimp salad she mixed up in a dishpan before putting it in smaller serving bowls for the table. After dinner and before the evening hunt, all of the kids would take off for the creek that ran below the house to play. One of our favorite games was Robin Hood and his merry men. There were lots of places to hide and ambush the King's men or if we were really brave, we would go to the barn on the other side of the creek and play in the hay."

After a good hunt, a family feast, and play day for the children, it was always back to work. Wildman, and his business partner Rexroth, kept Lester quite busy. They had hired him to farm, weld, mechanic, and whatever else they needed help with on their farms and farm equipment dealership. The partnership called their operation R & W, though the Keyes Valley Ranch continued to be known by its original name. There, and on farms all over the territory, Lester was making repairs on customers' harvesters, including the Rexroth's harvester, sixty miles away in the Temblor Mountains east of the Carrisa Plains.

Still, as on-the-go as Lester was for his employers, his wife and his children were of utmost importance to him. Hard work, marriage and family didn't mean he'd abandoned his mischievous side though - far from it. In fact, Barbara had grown to enjoy being the instigator of excitement as well, especially when the couple indulged in a date night either in town or in the country.

Like the night the couple attended a dance at the San Ardo Grange Hall. There, people from around the countryside had gathered for socialization and entertainment. The Grange in San Ardo happened to be across the street from Joe Alvarado's store and near the Evergreen Bar.

"Joe Alvarado's store was where you parked under his pepper trees to sit out there and neck," Lester recalled with a laugh." Used to go out there about supper time with your girlfriend and try and see if she wouldn't give you some."

Nearby, the Evergreen Bar was where, on that particular night, men named Jim McWilliams and Ed Paulson were having a drink. With Lester, no doubt encouraging her, Barbara caught a black and white cat, put it in Jim's pickup, and closed the door. The frightened cat hid under the seat.

Later, as Jim and Ed headed home, south of San Ardo near Ornack's, the cat jumped out from under the seat. In the dark it was hard to tell if the freaked out feline was a cat or a skunk. The pickup screeched over to the shoulder of the road and the men scrambled out of the truck. Jim squirmed out of his jacket, tossed it on the back of his pickup, then he and Ed tried to get the animal out of the cab. When the cat finally bolted out the door, the men got back in. As they drove home they left both the cat and Jim's jacket flying off to the side of the road.

When the men got home, Jim noticed his jacket was gone. He made it a point to find out who had put the cat in the pickup and when he did, he blamed Barbara for the mislaid jacket as well.

Though around that same time, Lester *could* have gone to town, to buy Jim a new jacket, at the same establishment where he had purchased his saddle a few years previously, the Paso Robles Mercantile, that's not why he went there one day. What he intended to do was buy a little something for his wife.

"They had everything in there," Lester remembered. "When the kids were young I went in to buy Barb a present. She needed a new bra so I went in there to the ladies part and this young gal come over to wait on me and wanted to know what I wanted. I told her I wanted a bra for my wife. She says, 'What size is she?'

"Hell, I don't know, about like that." Lester had cupped his hands in the shape of Barbara's breasts and held them out in front of himself, which embarrassed the salesgirl. "Her face got all red and she got all flustered, so May Tucker, who also worked at the Mercantile and knew that I was up to something, come over to see what was happenin' and she says, 'I'll take care of him'. May knew Barb so she helped me get the right size."

Such a helpful, and practical, husband – no long stemmed roses, no box of chocolates, no romantic card with written words of love and appreciation – but a bra - something Barbara had use for. However, since it was Lester doing the buying, one has to wonder if there was an ulterior motive for buying such a gift. Was his wife really so busy she couldn't find time to shop for herself as most women would prefer to do? Or, as suspected, was Lester's sudden spark of generosity fueled by his desire to cause some excitement? No matter, it was the thought that counted and Barbara was no doubt gracious, perhaps even pleased with the gift. Support for one another's needs, interests, hobbies, pursuits, and pastimes were normal, especially coming from Barbara. She was the foundation, the structural strength from which the family built itself. It was a role she embraced, one where she could not be outrivaled.

"When we moved back from Bakersfield, I was in the third grade, Chester was in second, and Margie was in kindergarten but Phillips School did not have a kindergarten so she got to stay home," Lester's daughter Regina said as she recalled the school house which could be seen from their home. "Phillips School was a two room school house, grades first through fourth. It sits up on the hill. We walked to school when the weather was nice and walked home. There is a foot bridge attached to the bridge that we use to walk on. We even walked on the outside top railing of the foot bridge just for the fun of it."

As if Barbara wasn't busy enough taking care of three children, a husband, parents, an upholstery and seamstress side-line, bowling, Grange meetings, and miscellaneous other organizations, she even volunteered to play a part in the local Phillips School's Parent Teacher Association's theatric production.

"One time Barb was in this P.T.A. school play," Lester said. "She had dyed her hair red and it changed her a lot."

Lester sat in the back of the audience to watch the play with two other men, Jim McWilliams and Ed Paulson. One of the men mentioned the hot red head on stage, who was probably wearing her fancy new bra under her costume, which gave Lester an idea.

"I sat there and messed with 'em. I said, 'Yeah, she's really somethin', isn't she? She probably could be had'."

The men joked back and forth about the 'good lookin' red head', right up until the end of the performance.

"I told these guys, 'I'll tell ya what. I'll bet ya fifteen dollars I sleep with her tonight'." Lester laughed. Did the men take him up on his bet? No. They weren't that gullible. They'd been pranked by the Rougeots before.

"The next morning we got up to leave for Yosemite and Barb's pillow was all red from the dye," Lester chuckled. It happened to be the beginning of trout season and time for the family's camping and fishing trip.

The annual excursion would become a tradition for the Rougeots, and their relatives which dates back to when Barbara and her siblings were little. Both Yosemite and Twin Lakes, west of Bridgeport, California, were favored fishing spots over the years but this particular trip the family headed for the floor of Yosemite Valley to camp out for a week.

"We'd leave the day before fishin' season, take the kids out of school 'cause we figured they'd learn more out in nature than they would in the classroom. Barb's parents and Raymond and Alice Miller and their three kids, Uncle Frank and Auntie Bobbie, Grandma's sister, Grandpa's brother, they all went over the years," Lester recalled. "On the way in we'd watch for downed trees then we'd gather wood for camp and cook fires for barbeque. Took all day to get there and set up tents. We'd take two camp sites and live there for a week. Ate fish every day.

"We had a camp stove we could cook fish on that were nine to twelve inches long but one year we caught fish fourteen to sixteen inches. They were too big for the fryin' pan so that's when we started to barbeque fish.

"One time when Chester was about six I cast his line in the water and hooked one and handed the pole to him and said, 'See if you can catch somethin',',."

When the pole Lester had handed to Chester started to dip and jerk Lester said, "You got one." Young Chester reeled in the fish. As it approached the shore the fish twisted and turned on the hook. Chester became very enthused about his catch.

"When the fish got about ten feet from shore Chester threw his pole to the side and jumped in the water after the fish," Lester said and laughed. "I had to grab him by the back of 'is shirt before he got in too deep.

"At Mirror Lake near Half Dome, you had to hide or the fish would see you. Oh, there was this one time, Barb and her sister, Alice, got into the whiskey while we was fishin' and they were lit, which was rare, when we got back. They really tied one on that day. It was so funny. And this other trip we had horseshoes pits in the snow one year.

"Up until 1968 they used to build a fire with big logs at the top of the Glacier Point in Yosemite. They called it the Fire Fall because every night about nine they'd push the fire over the face of Glacier Point, down three thousand feet and it looked like the falls was on fire."

YOSEMITE FIRE FALLS

"We used to go fishin' for blue gill in the creek behind the house, too," Lester's youngest daughter, Margie mentioned.

"There were swimmin' holes by the bridge at the house," Chester said. "The old bridge that they're replacin' now, it had a foot bridge on the north side. On the south side, all they had was this guard rail." Chester held his hands a few inches apart and indicated the size of the guard rail to be about the width of a school yard balance beam. "We'd wrap our legs around it, take our fishin' poles and you could see the frogs down there. It was a seventy-five or eighty foot drop. You could see the frogs down there so we'd catch frogs, we were always doin' stuff like that."

"And Mom took us swimming. Out to Shandon," Margie said. "Every summer."

"That's where we learned to swim," Chester said. "I had an orange swimsuit, a Speedo kind of thing. I'd dive off the diving board and go under water the full length and mom could see me under the water."

"We used to go clamming in Pismo, too," Margie said.

"Yeah, we used to get the kids up early in the morning," Lester said, "and take 'em to Pismo with us to clam. If we had the kids we'd get more clams."

"Yep, clams and abalone," Margie said. "The good old days."

"Then we'd bring 'em home and the kids would have to get ready to go to school."

"Mom would have to shuck 'em all," Margie said.

"Grandpa Rougeot always clammed too, didn't he?" Chester asked

"Yeah, my Grandfather Rougeot," Lester agreed, "he liked to clam."

CHESTER, MARGIE, AND LESTER ROUGEOT - 1956

CHESTER, MARGIE, AND BARBARA ROUGET - 1956

Besides their clamming excursions and the annual family fishing vacations, when Lester and Barbara were raising their children, a typical Sunday was also all about family. Road trips across the countryside took them to Hog Canyon, Big Stone, or Ranchita Canyon when their destination would either be Barbara's sister and brother-in-law's - the Miller Ranch in Parkfield, or to Lester's parents - the Rougeot Ranch in Indian Valley. If everyone piled in the car and drove up Proprieta in the Cholame area, the family was bound for Barbara's parents - the Hatch Ranch.

Along their chosen route for the day, Regina, Chester, and Margie rode in the back seat and were the official spotters. Lester at the wheel and Barbara riding shotgun, the couple would hone their shooting skills by target practicing at ground squirrels with their .22 caliber rifles. The children would scout out a squirrel, report its location, and If the rodent was on the driver's side it was Lester's shot, on the passenger side it was "Dead eye Barb" who took the bead.

That was a time when ranchers and farmers along the back country roads appreciated help with the elimination of ground squirrels. If left unchecked the destructive burrow dwellers multiplied rapidly and became more than just a nuisance. The squirrel's underground tunnel systems would lead to places where food was most plentiful such as hay barns and silos. Not only would they eat and contaminate massive quantities of livestock feed they undermined foundations, and made horse crippling holes in the land and farming fields.

DAVID KALAR ON TRACTOR – 1956

CHESTER ROUGEOT STANDS IN HAY FIELD
WITH HIS COUSIN DAVID KALAR ON TRACTOR - 1956

FARMING 1956

FARMING IN KEYES VALLEY - 1956

In addition to their regular Sunday excursions, the family liked to get together for yearly reunions which included relatives from both the country and the city.

"Back in the fifties, we had a Freeman/Nicklas reunion at the old Freeman home place in Hog Canyon where Babe and Susie Freeman lived," Lester's daughter Regina recalled. "Everyone went their own way and boys being boys they headed to the barn for some fun. Mark Young, being the city boy he was, followed along with his country cousins. Evidently, Mark was being Mark, and the boys got tired of his mouth and they took a rope and hung him from the barn rafters. One of the older girls, Lydia Freeman, heard him yelling and went to investigate. She found him hanging in the barn and got him down and chewed the other boys out."

"At the Freeman/Nicklas reunions, once my generation got old enough, we had baseball games - kids against the adults," Ken Freeman said. "We usually had a couple who were diehard baseball players and didn't like to lose. The adults were always horsing around, so you can imagine some of the spats that went on. Whenever Tom Freeman got up to bat, the outfield backed way up because they knew Tom would hit it really hard. What you have to understand is Tom was a big man. For him to get around the bases, he had to hit the ball into the next county."

"Tom never called me by my name," Lester's son, Chester commented and smiled. "He always called me, 'Chetter'. Oh and we used to tease my sister, her middle name's Francis. There was this 1950's movie with a mule in it named Francis so we teased Reg about being stubborn like a mule."

"We played baseball at the beach one time and the children were allowed to use their right arm to swing the bat and the adults had to swing with their left," Tom Freeman's wife, Emily explained and chuckled. "When Tom got up to bat, he hit the ball all the way into the ocean. The game had to take an intermission/break until the ball came back to shore with the tide. Seems the family forgot Tom was left handed."

"The Rega Freeman Ranch, stayed in the family until about 1960," Regina said, "when R.D. "Babe" Freeman, youngest son of Rega and Dovie Freeman, sold it to the Ernest Brothers." Thereafter the family gathered for reunions elsewhere.

It's plain to see Lester and his relatives made family a priority. That's not to say he didn't take his job seriously, as well. He did. Lester took pride in his reliability and ingenuity.

"Wildman's brochure there," Lester said and pointed to a bright red pamphlet among family photographs, "is more than fifty years old. I was the one that drove the experimental model of that thing. International Harvester's brochure, for Model 151, featured Lester as operator. "That's me on the brochure there."

Wildman knew what he was doing when he hired Lester to test drive the latest and greatest harvester money could buy. More than just an experienced farm hand, Lester was resourceful. Give

Lester a project and he was off and running. Where others might hit snags or run into insurmountable obstacles, not Lester. His proven ability to improvise and refusal to accept that there was a problem served Lester by allowing him to move on and accomplish what others said couldn't be done. Problem? What problem? And that's likely the reason he was given his next assignment.

"The harvester that Wildman got from the factory was the second one made, International's Model 151 Serial Number 502, 1959. The serial numbers started with 501, this one was 502. That's why I called it my 'drunkin' harvester'," Lester said. "That's when they come out with the four way leveler. It was an experimental harvester and I was the one who would find out if there were any bugs in it. In fact, the only thing I could find wrong with that harvester, you couldn't hear nothin' but that dang pitman down there. The pitman is the part that runs the knife."

McCORMICK®
No. 151 Hillside combine
- full leveling or side leveling models
  - both systems fully automatic

INTERNATIONAL HARVESTER

LESTER ROUGEOT
ON INTERNATIONAL HARVESTER'S MODEL 151 BROCHURE
1959

In communication with International's headquarters, Lester reported his findings. "I told 'em that pitman, if you can get it to where it doesn't make all that racket, it'd be a pleasure to drive this.

The guy says, 'Well if you can tear it up we'll have to build a new one'. So I said, 'Do you care how I do it?' and the guy says, "No, anyway you want'.

and across slopes...

Extra heavy rear axle and spindles are built to take the twists and strain of hillside combining, day after day, season after season. Husky tubular frame extends from front to rear axle on the side leveling model (below), while the full leveling separator is supported on a rugged hinged truss-type frame.

Heavy, oil-damped pendulum senses changes in slope ... opens and closes hydraulic valves to leveling cylinders. Linkage from pendulum to valve is mechanical ... there are no electrical circuits, switches, or solenoids. Leveling action is silk-smooth. The pendulum barely cracks valves for slight slope changes ... opens them wide when the change is abrupt. Oil damping prevents "overcontrol." You'll operate this combine over roughest hills and never feel it lurch or sway.

3

LESTER ROUGEOT ON INTERNATIONAL HARVESTER'S
MODEL 151 BROCHURE - 1959

"So I drove up to this oak tree and run it up against the base of this tree pounded against it and all it'd do is break the grease fittings and the slip clutch kept slippin'. So then I run it into a bank and that didn't work, so then they come out with the 403. They changed the pitman and it'd make a racket, and I sat there drivin' one day and listening to it and watchin' it and I decided what I needed to do. I went to town and bought a seven cent washer and took it out there and put it where it came together to keep it from bouncin'. I stuck that in there and it worked."

The impressive condition of experimental equipment, after it had been given a brutal beating by Lester, convinced him of their quality. Forever more, he would be what his cousin, Ken Freeman, would call, "An International man", a man who would praise the superiority and performance of International's equipment out of tried and true testing and firsthand knowledge.

"My drunkin' harvester. Serial number five oh two," Lester repeated and had to explain the equipment's nickname. "You know, a 502 is when you're drunk."

Although sold on their quality Lester mentioned, "I said, 'no', when they wanted me to go to Arizona and go to work for them on the experimental farm."

"Lester was such an International man that the guys would bait him by talking about other great equipment brands and he would defend IH to the hilt," Ken said. "It was so much fun getting him going."

One day when Lester was at Wildman's dealership to get a part for the equipment he was repairing, he ran into a friend.

"Mervin Rotta come in and ordered a new pitman and I says, 'You don't have to order that. Hell, a washer only cost seven cents, get one of those'. Man, the parts department manager at Wildman's got mad at me. And I worked for 'em! I drove the low-bed for 'em too and they'd ask, 'Where you goin' today?' Just to get 'em goin' I'd say, 'Oh, Pig Avenue'. That's what I'd tell 'em for Hog Canyon, and Rabbit Avenue for Hare Canyon, Wine Avenue for Vineyard Canyon. They never knew where I was goin'." Lester laughed.

Did he kid them with a straight face? Oh yeah. Could he have given them a straight answer if he'd tried? Doubtful. However, when it came to doing right by a friend or a customer, as with the seven cent washer versus an unnecessary and expensive pitman purchase, leave it to Lester to behave honorably. He may have made the manager mad, because the company lost a sale, but Lester knew how to be a good friend.

As with Ole Viborg, who at the time was a twenty-four year old Danish exchange student.

"After WWII, Denmark was still using horses for farming," Ole stated. "I'd come to learn how to use new equipment."

Though Ole had spent the previous several months milking one hundred cows in Solvang he wanted to learn about farming as well. He obtained the permission he needed from Denmark to take a job east of Paso Robles.

"Fred Nielson leased the Keyes Valley Ranch for alfalfa," Ole informed. "I was moving irrigation pipe with a 1949 Ford." The alfalfa fields appeared to be endless to Ole. Six miles out, seven miles, eight miles, then ten miles out and Ole says, "I got a little bit scared. I'd never been that far off road so I thought I'd go one more hill and that's when I ran into Lester. He was driving the harvester."

"When Ole first come over this hill he looked like he was kinda lost or lookin' for somethin'," Lester said. "It was hotter than hell that day."

"Lester said, 'You look like you need a drink,' and he gave me his canvas bag of water," Ole recalled. "We've been friends ever since."

Although Ole went back to Denmark, then to Canada, he returned, when the required two years was up, to marry his girlfriend, in Paso Robles and settle.

"Ole met Sandy at a Grange dance in Atascadero," Lester remembered with a smile.

The Viborgs and Lester continue to enjoy each other's company over Grange breakfasts or at Joe's Place, a favored restaurant.

"Five or six years after I'd been farmin' for Wildman, oh maybe in 1960 or 1961," Lester said, 'we bought this seed, it was two years out from bein' certified, ya know, pure seed, White Federation. You always try and upgrade your seed, ya know. And I planted it and sold one hundred tons to the Miller brothers and thirty-five tons to Ralph Shaw 'cause they'd never seen wheat that was so clean go through the harvester."

Lester took pride in his work. To make improvements wherever he worked was the way he operated. Still, no matter how seriously he took his job, no matter how busy Lester's work schedule, he always tried to adapt and adjust the conditions so they'd be suitable enough to include his wife and his children. Time with his family was of great importance.

"Chester was drivin', he was about twelve or thirteen and Margie was with 'im in the pickup," Lester said. "The kids was followin' me. They were in an International four wheel drive. Had it low range and they got off road in the ditch. Up and back down they went 'til the engine died. Barb asked Margie, 'Were you scared' and she said, 'No I was on the uphill side'."

"I belonged to Bluebirds, Camp Fire Girls, and Horizon Club all through school," Regina began. "There were several years that Margie also belonged to the Camp Fire Girls and when we would have our father/daughter banquet, Dad couldn't go with both of us so he went with Margie and I asked my uncle, John Craspay, to be my dad for the night. We all had a great time.

It was a time when Lester's son, Chester, would go with his dad as much as he could.

"Dad taught me how to drive the harvester," Chester said.

"Yeah, Chester drove the harvester but he couldn't reach the pedals. So this one time I was behind him and Chester was drivin' it down to the gate. I hadn't got to the gate to open it yet and he couldn't stop it so he drove around in circles 'til I got there."

"I had my first helicopter ride one spring day when I was with Dad, too," Chester mentioned. "He had the grain crop sprayed for weeds."

Lester and Chester met the helicopter pilot at the back of the ranch where Chester was offered a ride to the front of the ranch on the Estrella River. Below them in the grain field, Chester could see his mom, Barbara, shooting Jack rabbits that ran out to the edge of the field as the chopper got close. She had her Parker Brothers double barreled sixteen gauge shotgun Lester had given her. The same shotgun Chester had begged his mother to let him shoot, a few years previously, that had landed him on his backside because of its recoil.

"Great Grandpa Rougeot had a .3030," Chester mentioned, "and he kept track of the deer he killed by makin' little

BARBARA ROUGEOT, DOROTHY HATCH, EVERETT HATCH,
WADE AND FRANK HATCH, BLANCHE MCCONNELL
YOSEMITE 1961

LESTER ROUGEOT AND ALICE MILLER
YOSEMITE 1962

notches in the stock with a pocketknife. He had eight notches on one side and Dad had notches all the way up one side of the wood and back down." Chester laughed.

"That gun had a history before Grandpa Rougeot had it," Lester said. "A guy killed himself with it and the sheriff got it then Grandpa got it, then I got it, now Chester has it."

Though hunting and helicopter rides were considered the good times, there was one particular activity that somewhat disagreed with Lester's son, Chester. It was 1962, a time in a growing fourteen year old boy's life when he feels awkward and self-conscious.

"There was a U.S.O. building south of the park in Paso Robles and it was sort of a rite of passage for eighth graders to go, once a week, to learn ballroom dancing," Chester said and grimaced. "We had to learn the fox trot, the waltz, the promenade and all those different dances."

Though young Chester wasn't thrilled about the class, he said the old U.S.O. building was exciting. "There were all these nooks and crannies and hidden alcoves to explore."

Since then the U.S.O. building, once used for downtime and dances for soldiers and the community at large, has been torn down. When it was still standing it was a place where people met to socialize, smoke, get loose, and laugh.

"When we'd have a party in the old U.S.O. building behind San Miguel mission, the Brothers and Fathers, they'd smoke and drink with ya but they wouldn't dance," Lester said and chuckled. "Oh, I laughed when the women tried to get 'em to dance with 'em. Them women turned into a bunch of teasers. It was so funny."

Not that life was all sweet and no sweat. There were many days of laborious grind and grime. That's what made the celebrations so special. All that hard work meant merriment was merited and relished.

"About 1963 at the annual Freeman/Nicklas family reunion held at Clarence and Thelma Freeman Rougeot's Ranch in Indian Valley, the Freeman and Nicklas clan gathered for their yearly get together," Lester's daughter, Regina recalled. "Now, if you've ever been to one of these events, there are some routine things to expect. Country and City cousins, don't mix too well and things seem to just happen in the most unexpected ways. In the front bedroom of the

Rougeot home, you can hear Mark Young, from the city, explaining the finer points of magic to Nancy Lewis, half city half country. Mark would say, 'Nowwww, Nancy, you watch carefully at what I am about to do.' This goes on for about a half hour before Nancy makes her escape.

"The adults can be found around the barbeque pit with drinks in their hand seeing who can tell the biggest whopper, and believe me the Freeman/Nicklas bunch is known for them. At the other side of the house under the shade trees, you will find some of the teenagers engrossed in a high stakes, penny poker game and Uncle Babe Freeman watching over the action giving advice on the next play.

"After everyone gets their fill of the wonderful food, different groups spread out over the area around the house talking and catching up on what is going on in the family. You can find a baseball game being formed in the front field. Some of the kids are down below the corrals playing in the horse trough.

"This particular time, John and Sharon Freeman, Darlene Craspay, and I were at the horse trough trying to catch the gold fish and frogs that lived in the water. Darlene had been running her mouth and was bent over the trough trying to tell the rest how it is done. The opportunity presented itself and I upended Darlene head first into the horse trough. She came out spitting and sputtering, everyone but Darlene was laughing their heads off. Years later John and Sharon were still talking about this incident," recalled Regina.

It wasn't that the Rougeot children were mean. They just had their own definition of fair-dealings and entertainment. Fruit and nuts don't fall from the tree, as they say.

"The last time we had a family reunion," Regina began, "it was probably about the Spring of 1964, a group of "cousins" decided to take off and go up to the Mustang to see the snow. Frank Freeman had his jeep so with Frank driving, my brother Chester, John Craspay, Jr. and I hoped in. Well, Mark Young decided he was going to go too. So up the road we went to see the snow that had fallen the day before.

"On the way, we passed a natural fresh water spring beside the road and decided to stop for a drink on the way back. After turning around and heading back to the ranch, Frank pulled over at the spring and everyone piled out taking turns getting a drink. Mark asked where the cup was and we explained to our city cousin that you had to get down on all fours and drink that way. Being the sport he seemed to be, down on all fours he went. Now Mark was a little on the heavy side so this process took some time. While he was drinking his fill of the cool water, the rest of us ran for the Jeep and jumped in and away we went up around the corner. We finally stopped once we were out of view and waited to see how long it would take for Mark to catch up. Here he came just a huffing and puffing and threatening to tell his grandmother, my grandmother's sister Ona Belew, on us. We told him to go ahead and he could just walk the rest of the way back."

Nothing like the fear of being abandoned, culled from the herd, left to die alone and lost in wilderness to make a kid cooperate.

Regina continued, "We never heard any repercussions from this incident."

"It would have been November or December 1963, on the way past the Parkfield cemetery up the mountain, southwest Parkfield to the Hillman ranch," Lester's son, Chester began. "I was with my cousin, Harry Miller, and we were in the Jeep when I spotted this Jack rabbit."

Conveniently enough there was that shot gun of Chester's mother's, the double barrel Parker Brothers sixteen gauge, laying there in the Jeep. Chester thought he'd have a little fun when he told his six day younger cousin to grab the gun and shoot the rabbit.

"My cousin," Chester informed, "he was left handed. I told 'im, 'Shoot 'im. Pull both triggers. He's in the brush there you wanna make sure you hit 'im'."

Pow! Harry did as his trusted cousin had directed. He pulled both triggers. The gun blasted and Harry, well, "That ol' shotgun about kicked 'im out of the Jeep," Chester said and laughed.

Did Harry manage to hit the rabbit? Chester said, "Oh, yeah!"

Deer season at the Miller Ranch in Parkfield was when hunters came from all over California. There were places to camp out and drink where small children and women were not permitted.

Not surprisingly, Lester and his wife, Barbara, were not always known to comply with rules made up by others. Though they were aware of where the serious hunters were and went in the opposite direction, often they would hunt with Barbara's younger sister, Alice, and kids, Roger and Judy. Not a group that was known for their stealth like hunting tactics, the lighthearted and rowdy bunch would have been frowned upon in a camp for men, who considered themselves professional hunters.

At any rate after naptime, when the ranch had cooled down, Lester at the wheel of his Jeep, Barb and Alice riding shotgun, they cruised around while the children chattered. Lester sang and told stories. Barb and Alice spotted game and enjoyed the adventures. At the end of the day all the hunters met back at the ranch headquarters and much to the chagrin of some, it was often Lester's crew who came back with a nice buck. Even though the serious hunters had gotten up before daylight, hiked out long hot canyons, and drove over the thousand plus acres in search of their trophy buck they frequently came back empty handed with only tall tales of the one that got away.

"My mom and dad, Auntie Barbara and Uncle Lester, our families were very tight, close," Judy Miller said. "All six of us kids, we liked the same things."

"Judy's like my third daughter," Lester said.

"Yeah, well I'm adopted." Judy chuckled. "Regina, Chester, and Margie broke the ice by the time Roger and I came along, we could pretty much do anything," she divulged. "We could say things they could never say, do things. Everything was okay. Everything was accepted. Especially after Uncle Lester and Auntie Barbara's kids left home. After that, Uncle Lester and Auntie Barbara were always out there at my parent's house.

"Uncle Lester took us hunting behind the house on the other side of the creek, and my brother had hiccups. Uncle Lester was laughin' so hard. My mom would tell Auntie Barbara, 'Would you tell him to shut up'. He was constantly sayin' and doin' somethin'. Uncle Lester used to love to gig ya and get somethin' goin'. Whenever he took us hunting, he never told us to shut up. We could raise holy hell and Uncle Lester would be laughin' and singin' *The Whole Damn Family* or *She Lost her Hidey Ho'*.

"I had the game, Twister, and Uncle Lester used to win every game. He'd topple people over, get underneath 'em.

"I don't remember Uncle Lester ever saying 'no', ever. It would make him cry if he had to discipline us. No, he couldn't do that but usually when we were in trouble - he was in trouble - that's why.

"Uncle Lester was a challenge. It would take Auntie Barbara forever to reach a boiling point but once she did there were very few words spoken. He says they never had a fight. That's a bunch of crap – he never had a chance. She never raised her voice. She wouldn't make a big issue of things. She'd put her hand on his knee and he'd quit and pout.

"And this one time, maybe around 1963, when we were just kids, Uncle Lester took my brother and I out to Tom and Emily Freeman's to a Hungarian Hog slaughter. You know, where they put the straw down and drink the blood and all that?" Eyebrows lifted, disgust crossed Judy's face as she gave a shiver. "They laid the straw down and then the hog and they lit the straw and burnt the hair off. My brother, Roger couldn't stand blood. It was so gruesome and we were young. I was five or six. Roger he was seven or eight. We'll never forget that day. To this day you mention it to my brother and he gags."

Though, some adults might have protected young eyes from witnessing such a scene - not Lester. He liked to expose the children to the ways of the world because he himself was a man who related to the school of hard knocks more than a school with hardbacks. As far as Lester was concerned, to learn by doing and by firsthand experience was the best possible way to become truly educated and shrewd.

"Like with chewing tobacco," Judy said. "If you asked him for some chewing tobacco he'd give it to you. If you got sick, you got sick. You learned from him that way."

"One Christmas in Parkfield the kids were buggin' me to go quail huntin'," Lester reminisced. "Finally I said, 'Okay, I'll go'. So we went out and got in the jeep and I said, 'Stop'. I stood on my tip toes and there was a bunch of quail over there. I shot into the bunch of quail on this sand mound. Roger went over there gathered 'em up and said, 'Uncle Lester, you killed sixteen in one shot and two more the second shot'. We went down in the crick and at the end of the day we had seventy-seven quail."

"Ninety some quail that day," Chester corrected. "Finally ran outta shells. We cleaned 'em and ate 'em all. None went to waste. We ate the breast, the legs, we ate the wings."

The limit per person per day?

"Ten."

And still Chester claimed to be a "straight arrow". This from a man who admitted, on an F.F.A. trail ride, he once cracked himself up when he swatted a saddle sore, Nancy Carmenetti, on the rear, because she stood up in her stirrups to ease the pain.

Trail rides, fairs, campouts, sports, and meetings, organizations were big with the Rougeots. "I think we started with sheep about 1963," Regina began. "Chester got the F.F.A. flock, five ewes and a ram, and he got to keep any lambs. Margie had sheep up until she graduated in 1968. I never showed but dated a guy from Gilroy who had sheep and I ended up buying some Southdowns from my cousin, Wade, who had to sell his sheep when they moved to town."

"Southdowns," Chester repeated. "Reg didn't get into the sheep until she started goin' with Russell Rossi."

"He gave me my reserve champion," Margie interjected. "He gave that to me, which was nice. I think it was my cute personality."

Chester laughed at his sister Margie's comment. "I think Reg laid the ground work for ya," he suggested.

"I had a black sheep named 'Sambo'," Margie continued. "And there was this black ewe that had a lamb that wasn't real healthy, I got the lamb and I called her 'Phyllis'."

"When the kids were showing their sheep at the fair, the Atascadero Wranglerettes had a raffle for this Shetland pony," Lester said. "I bought one ticket, got home, unloaded the sheep, and the phone rang. Barb says, 'What are you gonna do with a Shetland pony?' and I says, 'Who you been drinkin' with? What Shetland pony?' I'd won the raffle but the kids were too big for it, so I went back to pick up this pony, and Shirley Moore, she ran the Wranglerettes, said, 'I'll give you one hundred fifty dollars for the pony or you can take it home'. I says, 'I'll take the money'. Never did bring that pony home."

A pony he had no use for. What he did bring home, or rather had delivered - the cord of firewood he later won in another raffle. Lucky Lester, firewood he could use.

It was September 21, 1964 when Lester's dad died in Paso Robles. Clarence was a few weeks shy of sixty-four years old.

"My dad had a bad heart and severe arthritis," Lester noted.

According to Lester, it was neither a shock, nor a surprise, when his father passed away. Lester took it upon himself to make sure his mother, Thelma got a ride to meetings and functions where her presence was needed. Where his father might have helped out, Lester stepped up to the plate, ready and willing to do right by his mother, when he felt she needed him most.

The transition from ranch wife to widow wasn't easy for Thelma. Left to make all the decisions about the ranch's future by herself, she was vulnerable and possibly disheartened by any unsolicited suggestions, proposals, or advice she may have gotten. But Lester wasn't a man who would manipulate or otherwise unduly influence Thelma's decisions. He wasn't there to put pressure on his mother for his personal gain. He was simply there for her, when she needed him. His support, his love, and his assistance were unwavering.

"After Grandpee died, I went to work for Jules Delwiche in 1965," Chester said. "Started out pickin' rocks out of fields."

Such a position in 2012, rock picker upper, might well be known as employment with 'job security'. Farm fields in the area were notorious for rocks that surfaced and seemingly grew out of nowhere. Lester's seventeen year old son, Chester worked hard that summer. Much like Lester and the generations before him had done, Chester gravitated toward farming and the great outdoors. Never mind the back-stressing labor, the dust, and the heat. These were men from pioneer families who had learned how to tolerate and thrive in less than optimal conditions. They had patience and perseverance on their side. Industrious and practical they figured out how to maximize their efforts.

Chester worked for Jules for the next twelve years. It was Jules who bought the Rougeot Ranch in Indian Valley, in the early '70's. That's when Chester and his bride, Louise, moved up to the ranch.

"I picked up rocks and also moved irrigation pipe in alfalfa, grain and sudan crops. Hauled hay, mowed alfalfa and barley. Hauled the hay to the barn I had Jules' girls help pick up the hay when they were older. They would drive the truck while I stacked the hay on the truck. Then I would take the truck to the barn and unload. I helped with the building of a feed mill and feedlot on the ranch. Jules grew out calves on sudan green chop, then finished them with feed mix from the mill. They were then sent to Bryant's Meat Packing in Paso Robles for processing and sold on the rail."

* * *

Providing experiences the children would benefit from was important to Lester and Barbara. They encouraged self-sufficiency, the exploration of talents, and the building of skills. Whenever possible the couple offered their children opportunities that would be both fun and at the same time would cultivate individuality and independence.

"Margie once said, 'My parents let me be me'," Lester added with a smile.

"Every summer I got to go to camp Tolaki in Lopez Canyon," Regina recalled. "For a week of camping and learning different nature, crafts, swimming, and taking overnight hikes. Several years Margie would go and Mom even worked in the kitchen helping with meals. I was probably a freshman in high school and Dad and Chester came to pick us girls up. I was at my tent packing up my stuff getting ready to leave and four of the senior girls asked me if I knew who was coming across the bridge. I asked which one they were talking about and they described the cowboy with the Stetson hat. They were saying what a hunk he was and how they would sure like to meet him and go out with him. I told them that it was my dad. But they wouldn't believe me until he came and helped me carry my stuff to the car."

Not that Regina needed to have validation of her dad's handsomeness. Nevertheless, as awkward as it may have been to have girls only slightly older than she, get all giddy over the presence of her dad, it didn't hurt to have others point out the hunk factor.

"It was 1966 when Grandpa Everett Hatch, Mom's dad, had gotten pretty sick," Regina stated. "He and Grandma agreed to move closer to Mom, so Mom could help both of them, with their needs."

"A house was moved from town," Lester said.

It was moved to Lester and Barbara's Whitley Gardens property where Everett Hatch, Barbara's dad, modified the house to suit he and Barbara's mom, Gracie. Not one to let someone else do all the work, Barbara helped her father with the remodeling. She was his right hand gal as they built a fireplace and prepared the newly relocated structure for occupancy.

"Grandpa was a skilled carpenter," Regina revealed. Many years later, Regina used her grandfather's antique wood working tools, in a Pioneer Day window display where, once again, she demonstrated her loyalty and commitment to the preservation of family heritage.

EVERETT HATCH'S TOOLS
DISPLAYED IN PIONEER DAY WINDOW

In preparation of recounting his past and providing pictures for his book, Lester combed his Whitley Gardens home. He dug through drawers and cabinets where some of the things inside had been stored for nearly sixty years. Had Lester's beloved wife, Barbara, been there she likely would have known right where everything was but Lester, though an organized man, felt a bit overwhelmed by the task. To search for a particular photograph or information meant hours of distraction when he came across other items of interest.

"I came across this folder with all these newspaper clippings of him and her," Lester said and jutted his chin toward his son, Chester and daughter, Margie. "When she was in high school Margie was the football princess and the F.F.A. sweetheart." Lester's chest puffed up with pride.

"Yeah, I got my looks from my mom and my personality from my dad," Margie revealed. "I played softball too."

"The Georgia girls they called themselves," Lester said. "They were good. Beat everybody."

"Boy, we had fun," Margie said, her posture at ease in the company of her father.

"Then in January, 1969, there was a flood in back of the house," Lester recalled. There in their Whitley Gardens home next to Estrella Creek, Lester and his wife, Barbara, watched the water rise. "It got about fifty feet from the house and it come up about two feet into the kids sheep shed. Barb and I was sleepin' and we heard the old bridge on Highway 46 wash out. The cement slab on the bottom there, on the East bound lane, slipped off and we heard it hit the water about eleven at night. They closed the highway about three thirty in the morning. People had to drive by our house and go over the old steel bridge to get over the river."

The second old bridge Lester spoke of is covered with steel framework, built in 1910, and still stands today. Though the county is considering tearing it down Lester has taken it upon himself to try to save the historical landmark. He recently wrote and submitted his argument in favor of keeping the bridge.

"My neighbor across the river, Charlie Yearwood, had his walnut orchard fill up with silt four feet deep during that flood. It woulda killed his trees. I was the trustee of his estate even though his wife was still there I was the one who let people come in and get the silt for their horse stalls. A guy came and wanted to buy a bunch of it and I told him, 'No,' 'cause I'd have to get a miner's permit to sell it."

Six months later, on Lester's forty-fourth July 20, 1969 birthday, an American spacecraft, Apollo 11 landed on the moon, after which astronaut, Neil Armstrong was the first man to walk on the cratered planet. The topic became one Lester had fun with. "My neighbor, Jim McWilliams had his birthday the day after mine. He used to say, 'They landed on the moon on my birthday,' and I'd say, 'No, they landed on *my* birthday'.

No doubt about it - times were changing.

"Dad's words were, 'God damn, the hell I am'," Regina explained as she told of the phone conversation between her new husband and Lester. "I had married my husband, Kelley, in August 1968. We moved to the mountains of Southwestern Virginia. By the following Spring I was expecting our first child. Kelley told me he wanted to be the one to tell my dad about being a grandfather and he said he knew exactly what he would say. Sure enough when we called to tell them the news, Kelley started laughing at Dad's response after he told Dad he was going to be a grandpa about December.

"When I was pregnant, we flew to California, in August, for a visit. I'd been away from home for a year. During the time I was gone, there were several changes being made. Dad went from a twenty-nine inch waist in 1968 to about a thirty-four inch waist in 1969. He told me I sure wasn't very big to be as far along as I was supposed to be. I lifted my shirt, patted my tummy and said I had an excuse for my extended tummy, what was his. Everyone started laughing and agreed I was a lot bigger than I looked with my maternity shirts on and teased Dad about his expanding waist.

"The baby was due the first of December, by the tenth, the folks decided they couldn't wait any longer and flew back on the sixteenth of December. Still no baby, we took Mom and Dad on a lot of country roads and showed them where we were thinking of building a home. Dad thought we were crazy to want to live so far out in the mountains. About midnight on the eighteenth of December the little guy decided it was time to make an entrance. Not being sure what was going on, Kelley came home after work and asked how I was doing. I said fine and for him to go on to sleep. After he was asleep I decided I had better get up. I went down the hallway where Mom and Dad were sleeping.

"After saying, 'Mom' a couple of times, I heard, 'Barb' and a thump. Dad had pushed Mom out of bed. Mom and I sat at the kitchen table timing my contractions and after an hour we decided we needed to get to the hospital. I walked by dad's room and told him it was time to go, all he could say, 'It's about damn time.'

"I woke Kelley up and it was funny watching him trying to get dressed and trying to help me get dressed. Dad jumped in the shower and told Kelley to come back and get him. Mom was cool and collected waiting at the door all dressed and riding shotgun in the back of the car. Every time I had a contraction I would squeeze Kelley's leg and he would go a little faster.

"Michael Kelley didn't arrive until about 2:30 p.m. December 19, 1969, weighing in at nine pounds eleven ounces and twenty and a half inches long. Dad and Kelley had gone to get someone to cover for Kelley at work and to leave his keys. When they got back they were greeted with a son and grandson. Three days later "Mikie" was brought home. Dad had a cold so he had to wear a mask to cover his nose and mouth. Still, he was bound and determined he was going to hold his grandson. Mom gave Michael his first bath."

Would being a forty-four year old grandfather calm Lester down and turn him into a fuddy-duddy old timer? Yeah, right. As evidenced in upcoming years, time and age actually seemed to kindle his wild side.

LESTER ROUGEOT ON A CABALLEROS TRAIL RIDE

7 – SOLD, SOLD, AND SOLD

The man could be taken out of Indian Valley but Indian Valley could never be taken out of the man. Indian Valley, the ranch, the land, and the people had always embraced Lester. It was his comfort zone, his sanctuary. Indian Valley was the one place that held Lester's heart, it was always the road that led to the place that felt like home.

Though he hadn't lived there for many years he had always counted on the ranch to be there for him and his children and their children. After all, land couldn't go anywhere. That would never change. Yet it did. And when it did, it was hard to believe. It was the one thing that was supposed to remain. The long established feeling of security that Lester felt for his special place on the planet – gone with the swipe of a pen.

Somehow, like looking through a cloud of dust, the world seemed different, the future not as clear as it once was. Although Lester had experienced disappointment and loss in his past, nothing saddened him quite like the sale of the family's Indian Valley ranch.

"My parents started the ranch with a hundred head of cows, a hundred head of calves, and sold calves each year," Lester said. He sat with his eyes fixed on an internal sight. "Eventually they had bought the bank loan and paid it off."

The Rougeot Ranch, all four thousand acres of it, sold in 1972 to Jules Delwiche for five hundred thousand dollars - half a million. That was a dark day for Lester. Indian Valley had contributed to his competence; it had confirmed his masculinity, his strengths, and his spirit. Not only had he grown from boy to man on that ranch, he had hoped generations to come would benefit from the land, as he had. For Lester, it wasn't the monetary value of the land that would be missed, it was the tradition, the heritage, and the character that could only be acquired from having a close relationship, a connection, and respect for the location where one felt at home.

Nevertheless, Lester wasn't a man who dwelled on the negative. The decision making power was out of his hands. Though he voiced his thoughts and opinions, he had the wisdom to forbear what he couldn't change. Whatever his mother's reasons – surely they were ones that weighed heavy on her heart as well.

At least Lester had the satisfaction of knowing his children knew Indian Valley. They had visited, helped out, hunted, and played there. Having his son and daughter-in-law live at the Indian Valley ranch after it sold, Lester knew they, and their daughter, Mary, his granddaughter, would form a strong affiliation for the land thus carry on the fond feelings and that deeply rooted sense of belonging that mattered so much to Lester.

"I was workin' for Jules Delwiche when Grandmee sold the ranch to 'im. I worked for 'im from 1965 until 1977," Chester said. "My wife, Louise, and daughter, Mary, and I moved to the Indian Valley Ranch after he bought it. Grandmee had already moved to the home she had purchased in Paso Robles. Jules had leased the ranch with an option to purchase which he did in 1975.

"Mary was two and went to school in Bradley for the 1976-1977 school year. Mary was born in Sierra Vista Hospital in San Luis Obispo, June 29, 1970. Louise was an aid at Bradley school and took Mary with her to school. This was like a preschool. Mary started school in Bradley and finished first grade in Cayucos. Then we moved to Cayucos and lived there until we moved to Idaho, April, 1977."

Right around the same time, the Rougeot's Indian Valley Ranch sold and after farming for Morrie Wildman for twenty plus years, since 1951, Lester went to work for him as a salesman in 1974. J.M. Wildman, Inc. was a Jeep, Oldsmobile, Pontiac, Buick, Opel, and Cadillac dealership at 3328 Spring Street. That's where I, Lester's biographer, met Lester for the first time in 1975. I had taken my CJ5 Jeep in for servicing and although he was not in the service or parts department I remember Lester greeting me and was very helpful in getting me the attention I needed.

The following year, 1976, while I attended California Polytechnic State University, also known as Cal Poly, in San Luis Obispo, I was given an assignment for an Agricultural Sales and Service class known as Agricultural Business Management, ABM 201. Instructor Duane Seaberg told the class to interview someone in an agriculturally related business and he gave us criterion to work from.

Lester agreed to an interview and kindly allowed me to spend a day with him while he worked. It was a day of wide friendly smiles, big cigars - for Lester, not me - and a lot of laughs for both of us. Lester went all out to make sure I got the information I needed to succeed on my term paper. What I learned that day was that a clear and honest presentation of benefits to the buyer was forefront. Lester's method of selling was to find out a potential customer's needs and desires then meet them, often going above and beyond the call of duty. Consequently, Lester acquired a customer base that repeatedly turned to him for their purchases.

That day, Lester taught me, if the customer couldn't come to him, he'd go to them. He was not the type to pace the showroom floor. We went to Templeton to let a woman test drive a Cadillac that day. Although the husband had already looked the car over, the ultimate decision maker was the wife. We took the car to her, just as we did for people in Indian Valley, and downtown Paso Robles. By going out of his way to give customers that little something extra, more than they would expect, Lester's sincere enthusiasm and belief in his product encouraged people to buy.

When asked, Lester let on that his favorite part of the job wasn't all about making a sale; it was the interaction with the different people.

"No matter what they appear to be on the outside," he said, "you treat everyone equally."

With Lester's help the evaluation of my term paper was scored with a sixty-five out of sixty possible points. I sent him the A+ results along with a letter that said, "We did it!" and together we had.

Point of interest: It was, in part, because of that term paper that I am the one who is blessed to have written Lester's book. He had saved the paper for the past thirty-seven years, had it on his kitchen table, and was talking to his son Chester about looking me up in the Cal Poly directory.

Turned out that wasn't necessary because, as fate would have it, Lester's housekeeper, Jane Holton, had come by that day and noticed my name on the term paper and she said, "Hey, I know her." Jane had once been a neighbor of mine in the Santa Lucia Mountains, we had recently reacquainted and became friends on Facebook. She let me know Lester was looking for me. All four of us - Jane, Lester, Chester, and I met for breakfast, and the rest is now printed history. Thanks, Jane!

JANE HOLTON AND LESTER ROUGEOT
AT AN EL PASO DE ROBLES GRANGE #555 PANCAKE BREAKFAST
SPRING 2012

Okay, back to the story...

Not surprisingly, Lester was very successful in his job at Wildman's. He told of a day when he sold three vehicles in fifteen minutes.

"Gave 'em all the keys to go for test drives," Lester said, "and they all came back at the same time and wanted to buy." Lester, along with his coworkers, had to scramble to get all the paperwork done in a timely manner.

Unfortunately, the rapid succession of sales - sold, sold, and sold in fifteen minutes - along with all the other sales Lester managed to make, didn't set well with some of the other salesmen. They began to whine to Jerry Wildman. The fact that they weren't as skilled at sales as Lester wasn't the complaint. They never bothered to study Lester's talented salesmanship. They merely protested.

When Lester caught wind of their objections he decided to give them a chance, He held back. For two weeks, every time a potential customer came in, Lester disappeared into a car and off the grounds completely. Unfortunately for the dealership, the other salesmen didn't manage to make one single sale in those two weeks. It was Morrie Wildman who finally went to Lester to see what the problem was. Upon learning what was going on, he insisted Lester get back to what he did so well, much to the annoyance of fellow salesmen. And, sure enough, that's when sales began to pick up again. Lester stayed on at Wildman's until he retired - the first time - in 1977.

LESTER AND BARBARA ROUGEOT - 1976

LESTER ROUGEOT – 1978

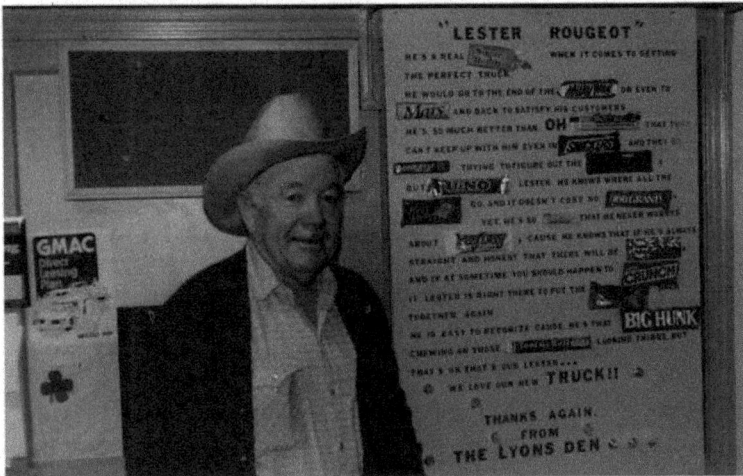

CUSTOMERS APPRECIATE LESTER ROUGEOT
WITH A SIGN MADE OF CANDY BARS

Within weeks of retirement Lester was approached by John Palla to work for Palla Equipment.

"Barb says, "You're a damn fool if you don't go to work for him," Lester revealed.

Lester's wife, Barbara, knew her husband well. She had wondered what he planned to do with his time if he wasn't working. "You don't like to travel," she said. "You don't like to sit around."

As a result, retirement lasted a whopping six weeks before Lester decided to go to work as a salesman for Palla Equipment in Paso Robles. "I sold five harvesters, the first year," Lester stated matter-of-factly. "That was more than the dealership sold in the previous twelve years."

The International Man had expanded his persona into a GMC Man as well. Many farm and ranch trucks around the area had been purchased with Lester's help. Customers admired and trusted Lester; he knew what he was talking about, he steered people right, he saw to their needs. Some regulars liked him so much they created a sign made of written words and candy bars to show their appreciation.

In October of 1980, I too, turned to Lester. Though I was just twenty-four years old and I'd never purchased a new vehicle, Lester made it easy. Soon, I drove away in my blue Heavy Half GMC pickup, a happy customer.

MICHELE OKSEN AND LESTER ROUGEOT - 1980

As Chester steered his pickup past the places where Lester and his parents and grandparents had lived, the tires hummed while peaceful terrain, gentle slopes viewed from the pickup window, soothed the soul. Shirt pockets full of note pads, pens, and glasses Lester removed his hat and leaned back to enjoy the scenery as he reminisced about the 1980s.

"When I was workin' for Palla, one time before we went to lunch, I was in ol' Richard Pacheco's office, you know he had these damn toothpicks," Lester remembered as he thought back. "He had a whole drawer full of 'em that he'd gotten at restaurants, ya know, when he was in there. So, he took 'em out and he had 'em stacked there on his desk. So I took 'em and put 'em in the middle of the floor there in his office and he said, 'what are you doin?' and I says I'm gonna build me a fire. It's a little cold in here." Lester laughed at the memory as his head tipped back and his straw hat bumped the headrest in his son's pickup. "And ol' Richard says, 'Don't you light that thing on fire'. And I just reached down there and lit it afire. Ol' Richard tried to stomp it out, then grabbed some of it and threw it in the wastebasket and set it afire."

"Richard Pacheco's office was at the Black Oak Liquor store, where Big Bubba's Barbeque is now," Chester informed as he drove the pickup along the back roads of San Miguel.

"We'd go to lunch every day," Lester recalled. "Richard would buy one day I'd buy the next."

Of course lunch was never just a meal with Lester. Every chance he got he liked to test the limits of his unique brand of comedy - just in case there was any excitement to be had.

"One day, we went to the Black Oak and I pulled out a hundred dollar bill and put it on the counter and asked the waitress what she'd do for it and she said, 'Lester, would you put that away. Put that away.' I says, no, no, no. I just wanna know if you'd do anything for it."

While Lester's, buddy, Richard paid for lunch everyone near Lester was laughing.

"This good lookin' gal in the nut part asked, 'What are you guys doin' in there?' Oh, we was just laughin' about the price of it. What d'you charge?"

The most fun for Lester was when he lured someone into playing along. When the salesgirl in the Black Oak's almond store answered, "Three hundred dollars", well, that was like fanning a fire. Let the smoke blowing begin.

"Three hundred dollars?" Lester gasped then asked, "How do you want it in hundreds or twenties?"

"Hundreds."

"I turned to Richard and says, 'Hey have you got a couple hundred dollars you could loan me?' He says, 'Yeah.' He reached in his pocket, 'Here's two hundred dollars'. So I hand it to her. She looks up and says, 'Well, I can't go right now I gotta work for another thirty-five minutes'."

The heat was on but the practical joke continued, somewhat like an adult version of a childhood dare. Who will take it the furthest? Who will be the naughtiest? Who will cry, 'uncle' first?

"Well, I says if I'm goin' for three hundred dollars I'm goin' now 'cause I gotta go back to work myself."

Back and forth Lester and the salesgirl haggled until she handed back the money.

"So we started out the door and I says, 'Richard, here's your two hundred dollars back.' He says, 'What was you doin'?' Well I asked her how much she charged and she said three hundred dollars. Ol' Richard says, 'That was *my* money.' And I says, 'Yeah, and I'd of thanked you for it.' I was always doin' stuff like that to 'im."

After Lester's story, the question had to be asked.

"What would you have done if she would have taken you up on your offer, Lester?"

"Everybody always asks what I'd do if one of these gals takes me up on it," Lester answered. "I say, 'Oh hell that's easy. I'd just tell 'em I had a headache'."

When out on the town with Lester, surprising situations were more likely than not. One could never guess what might enter Lester mind and come out his mouth. As several folks noted over the years – it's in his eyes. Look through the blue and the gears are in there spinning away. Not - *will* he come up with something but, *what* will he come up with next? That was, and still is, the question. Lester's niece, Judy Miller put it this way, "When Uncle Lester's around you never knew what was gonna be on your plate, you never knew what he was gonna do next."

MARGIE, BARBARA, LESTER, JUDY

"In San Luis after a Native Sons meeting, I was District Deputy, had installed their officers that night, and Earl Lewis and Al Fall said, 'We'll take you out and have a drink.' McClintock's was like a swarm of bees, all them college kids, so I said, 'Hell let's go someplace else', so we went to a place I says, 'What the hell are we doin' here? This is worse than the Elkhorn in San Miguel. Look at all these scuz buds in here."

"Would you shut up?" one of Lester's companions said.

"So we had a drink there then wound up over at Motel Inn. We got in there and there was six seats left at the bar. This brunette next to me was talkin' to this guy and I thought, *Man he's a dickhead what the hell is she doin' with that guy?*

Though he judged the man who was trying to impress the dark haired beauty, to be unworthy of her attention, Lester was a bighearted man who didn't like to call a guy a dickhead, to his face. Instead he would bait Dickhead into a bet. The flip of a coin and justice would be served.

"I had a silver dollar," Lester mentioned, "that I could win with ninety percent of the time."

When Lester finally addressed Dickhead he said, "Hey, I'll tell you what I'll do. I'll match you for your girlfriend here. If you win I'll give you five bucks, if you lose I get her. He says, 'Naw, I'll match you for one of these others.' There was a redhead and a blonde there. So I told 'im, 'No, if I'm gonna match I wanna match for this one'."

The bar banter made the bartender ask what was going on and Lester explained matter-of-factly he was, "Just matchin' this guy for his girlfriend."

Much to Lester's delight it turned out the brunette was a deputy sheriff's wife. "I danced with all three of them women for an hour and a half. Dancin' the Cha-cha, cheek to cheek."

Again, after the story was told an obvious question demanded to be asked.

"Where was Barbara?"

"Oh, I'd dropped her off at a Cowbelle's trail ride that day so she wasn't around. I told 'er all about it later."

And the lucky silver dollar? Beware when that thing came out. Lester was known to flip his coin for just about anything. A meal – get the coin. A line at the barbershop - pull out the coin. When Lester's friend, Johnny Perry, didn't go for that idea Lester tried to trick him into losing his place in line by pointing out a pretty woman on the street, who wasn't really there.

LESTER ROUGEOT – BARBEQUE MASTER

It was one thing to be wise to the ways of Lester. It was quite another thing to be at all gullible or ill-advised of his tendencies.

"One time we was havin' this barbeque and Margie had this friend over," Lester began. "He was a dentist, watchin' me plant radish seeds."

"What are you doing?" asked Margie's dentist friend.

"Oh, I'm just plantin' a few radishes."

"How long before they're ready to eat?"

"Oh, by tomorrow they'll be some ready."

"Really?"

"Oh sure," Lester said with sincerity written all over his face. "This ground is real fertile. And I put this stuff on my hands and when I touch the seeds it gets on 'em. Makes 'em grow real fast."

"Wow, amazing."

"Isn't it though?"

The family commenced with their get together. Barbecued beef cooked by Lester, an enjoyable evening spent visiting and informing those who didn't know any better how to cultivate miracle radishes.

Early the next morning before anyone else was up Lester snuck into the kitchen and raided the refrigerator. Careful not to make any noise, he grabbed a bag, gently closed the refrigerator, and slipped out the door.

Once he was in the garden, he glanced back at the house to see if anyone had seen him, all was quiet. Knees in the dirt he leaned over and made holes in his fertile soil. From the produce bag that had come out of the refrigerator, he pulled a bunch of radishes. One by one he put them in the holes then tamped the dirt around each one leaving the greens unburied. Sprinkle a little water over the top and poof – wonder upon wonder – ready to pluck from Mother Earth and eat.

Are people really so far removed from where their food comes from that Lester could make a dentist believe radishes grow from seed to an edible root overnight?

Sadly, the answer is, 'Yes', some really are.

"The next morning this guy walked out there and he says, 'Oh, they really did come up' and I says, 'I told ya'."

"That's hard to believe," the dentist said.

"Well, that's how I get it done," Lester said. By then the radish tops had started to wilt so Lester figured he might just as well let the guy off the hook.

"I finally told 'im the truth."

"Hey," Margie interjected, "I didn't say my friend was bright."

Not that Lester, or his children, only picked on outsiders. Oh, no. The Rougeots were just as likely, if not more so, to tease each other. Equal opportunity pranksters.

MARGIE TICKLES HER DAD'S NOSE
WITH A BLADE OF WILD GRASS WHILE HE NAPS

"One time, when we met to go to Twin Lakes, I met them, Judy, Mom, and Dad at Highway 46 and Interstate 5," Margie said, "and Dad got in the car with me and Judy and Mom went on their merry way 'cause Dad was sick so he'd be fallin' asleep. As we were goin' up 5, where this one area where there's Tule elk, and we always looked for 'em, he'd start to wake up and I'd go, 'Dad! There's one, there's one'. Dad would sit up and look around for the elk."

"Where?" Lester would ask. "Where?"

"Oh, you just missed it," Margie would tell her father.

By the second time Margie pulled the pretend elk sighting on her dad, he'd figured it out. He was, after all, the grandest master and mentor of such goings on.

"We were always doin' stuff like that," Margie said and laughed. "Like when Mom caught a horny toad and held it up for Dad to see. 'Look', Mom said and Dad was gone."

"Bees and horny toads," Chester said. "Dad hates 'em."

Imagine that – Lester Rougeot, Mr. Macho himself, afraid of a little ol' horny toad, a gentle and harmless, albeit a creepy and prehistoric looking lizard, that preys on bugs and can squirt blood from its eyes when threatened.

"Mom thought that was the funniest thing," Margie said.

Though Lester and Barbara's children had long since grown up, married, moved away, and had their own lives, they made it a point to keep in contact and visit whenever possible. Still, family members, including Lester and Barbara, had full lives, busy, demanding, and occupied with professions, organizations, and hobbies. Two of Barbara's preferred activities for her leisure time were bowling and gambling. Proof of her partiality for bowling – trophies, plaques, and awards for her winning scores – embellished their home. Evidence of her zeal for gambling – that was different. That was something she liked to hold close to her vest.

"Auntie Barbara loved to go gambling. We started goin' on the bus on these gambling trips," Judy Miller said. "Uncle Lester wouldn't go and Auntie Barbara says, 'We don't want you to go'. The secret was, whatever money Auntie Barbara had, she wasn't gonna tell Uncle Lester, with whatever money she won, whatever money she came home with, she wasn't gonna tell 'im. So he'd always say to me, 'How much money did Barb take?'

"Reno, Laughlin, Auntie Barbara put money in every compartment. She'd always get double diamonds, four hundred quarters, and say, 'Don't tell Lester'. She'd get home and he'd ask, 'How much money'd you win?' and she'd say, 'I'm not gonna tell ya', so one time he said, 'I'm goin".

"So he went this one time, and there's Uncle Lester at the bottom of escalator at the Riverside. We were goin' up the escalator with Auntie Barbara to go gamble. And here's those girls goin' on their shift in their short skirts and fish net stockings. Uncle Lester waited for them to get on the escalator so he could stand at the bottom and watch 'em go up."

To stand at the lowest level of the escalator inside the Riverside Casino, it was the same tactic as being down in the mechanic's pit at Paso Robles High School, when Lester went there. Some things never change.

"Auntie Barbara loved to gamble and she loved the secrecy of the money," Judy divulged. "It was like a game to her but I think Uncle Lester got his tail twisted over it. She never spent money though. The only money she'd spend was at the Indian casino and she'd buy cartons of cigarettes 'cause they were cheap there."

Casinos and gambling just weren't Lester's thing. And that was okay. While Barbara was away pulling handles on one-armed bandits, otherwise known as slot machines, Lester was busy pulling legs of friends and associates.

"You treat everyone equal," Lester declared once again. And he does - consistently. Fair-minded and non-discriminatory in his treatment of others, there is no one exempt from his signature brand of humor, or his inclination to instigate excitement.

While at one of the El Paso de Robles Grange pancake breakfasts Spring 2012, Lester's niece, Judy Miller, leaned forward and rested her forearms on one of the many dining tables. A 4-H member came by and offered coffee and a steaming plate of scrambled eggs, bacon, and pancakes, which Judy politely declined, much to the disappointment of the young man who was eager to be of service while he earned points toward advancement.

Chester had his back to the dining room as he dispensed batter onto the grill in perfect rounds. Lester had people in the corner of the room in stitches. Lester too, laughed with gusto, in his element.

Judy looked to either side of herself, then over her shoulder to see who was listening before she continued in a hushed tone. "I always called Uncle Lester about the same time every night," she said. "He thought it was me and he didn't have caller ID. He answered the phone and said something filthy, thinkin' it was me but it wasn't."

Lester, who had just been laughing it up, with folks who sat and ate in the corner of the room, approached Judy with a sheepish expression on his face. He knew his niece had the real scoop on him and he knew Judy wasn't one to sugar coat things. She, much like her

Auntie Barbara, had a 'tell it like it is' approach. Lester was sure Judy was spilling the beans, revealing the crusty baked on grit at the bottom of the pot. And he was right.

"Judy, she looks after me," Lester acknowledged. He looked up and waved with enthusiasm as incoming Grange pancake breakfast regulars walked in the door. The smell of hotcakes, bacon and coffee, along with the clatter of kitchen activity, and the chatter of happy people filled the room.

"That's true. I look after 'im. Like Regina, she's in Virginia now, but she stayed and helped with my mom and everything. When Uncle Lester gets sick, I get 'im. I cook, get groceries, and take care of 'im," Judy said with a grin. "And if they can't find him, they call me. Every night he called me, started years ago when I moved here. It was a big deal for him to call me or hear from me." Judy smirked. "I was to call him 'cause supposedly he was watchin' out for me. Auntie Barbara would say, 'You better call Judy, she hasn't called yet'. So this one time I called and Uncle Lester answered sayin' somethin' he shouldn't have and it wasn't me." Judy laughed as she nodded her head and leaned back in her chair. "It was a woman applyin' to work at the grange hall, a nice religious lady. He had to apologize profusely. He's a little devil. Most people don't know this side of him."

"Hey, I go to church," Lester claimed with a straight face. "I go to the round church. That's where the devil can't corner ya." He laughed.

Judy rolled her eyes. "I remember my Aunt telling Uncle Lester that he needed to be more careful with what he said, and she said he got what he deserved for being so such a smarty pants. This is what triggered my Auntie Barbara and I to buy Uncle Lester, for his birthday, telephones with caller ID. So on July 20, 2010, he got his birthday present. Even though she was gone, she and I planned this and I bought them and showed them to her in June 2010 and she thought it was the greatest birthday present, so he would not make a fool of himself."

So, what had Lester said when the decent and decorous woman had called for an interview? Well, it could have been any number of things. Lester wasn't certain, as it was far from the only time he answered his phone saying something others might have interpreted as improper. Whenever Lester thought he knew who was on the other end of the line, he tended to answer his calls by saying things like, "Lester's house of ill-repute," or, "Lester's cathouse," or, other times he'd say something in a husky provocative tone like, "What are you wearing?'".

Call the Rougeot household and Lester might even answer with a yodel. Then there's always the chance he might belt out a song such as, *She's Sellin' What She Used to Give Away.*

She's Sellin' What She Used to Give Away

Written by Buster Jones 1938, Performed by Buddy Jones

Well, a redheaded gal lived down on the farm
She messed around but didn't mean no harm
She worked in the fields but didn't make no dough
Still held on to her hi-de-ho
And now she's selling, what she used to give away
She went to the city with a dollar or two
Soon found out that jobs were few
Her money gave out and her spirits went low
But she still held on to her hi-de-ho
And now she's selling, what she used to give away
Well, things got better, then she wanted some more
She opened up a honky tonk right next door
Whiskey went up and beer went low
But she still held on to her hi-de-ho
And now she's selling, what she used to give away
She started making money, selling gin and ale
The place was raided and she went to jail
She got out and was ready to go
Hangin' right on to her hi-de-ho
And now she's selling, what she used to give away I mean,
she's selling, what she used to give away

"Dad's songs were funny to us kids," the Grange's official flapjack flipper, Chester said wielding a spatula and wearing a cowboy hat, boots, and an apron. "They may not be appropriate today. Like, *The Whole Damn Family.* Dad used to sing that when we were goin' some place. We'd be in the back seat of the car laughin' at 'im."

That's one of the things Lester does best. He keeps people laughing. It's his way to accentuate a positive aspect of life - humor. And *The Whole Damn Family*, the catchy tune he'd long ago burned into his brain at his cousins', Tom and Emily Freeman's ranch, the mere mention of it was all it took for Lester to break into song.

The Whole Damn Family

In the 1930's this song was performed by Bill Cox.
The following lyrics are Lester Rougeot's version.

Oh, I lived on a little farm
as peacefully as could be
until one day a man moved in
and brought his family.
There was Old Man Damn, Old Miss Damn,
and the Damn kids, two or three
Well, I'll be damned and you'll be damned
and the whole Damn family.
Old lady Damn she was quite stout
she weighed three hundred pounds.
She sat down in my rockin' chair
and broke the damn thing down
I wish they were in Halifax
That's where they ought to be
Well, I'll be damned and you'll be damned,
and the whole Damn family.
They pulled up in my old tin Ford.
They thought they'd take a stroll.
They hit my yellow Tom cat,
you should have seen him roll
I wish they were in Halifax.
That's where they outta be.
Well I'll be damned and you'll be damned
and the whole Damn family

GRANGE FLOAT IN THE PIONEER DAY PARADE
PASO ROBLES - 1934

"In 1935, my sister, Sis, and I rode donkeys in the Pioneer Day Parade behind the Grange float," Lester said. "I was ten years old." He adjusted his straw cowboy hat exposing his blue eyes and a bit of forehead as he sat back in his chair at the long table inside the El Paso de Robles Grange Hall #555. He was ready to talk about a subject near and dear to the core of his being – life as a member of the Grange.

"I couldn't join the Grange until 1939, but Sis and I got to go in the parade with 'em in '35."

Mounted on donkeys, with no saddles or bridles, but rather ropes tied into makeshift halters, behind the Grange float Lester and Sis waved like celebrities at the people who watched the parade from the street. It was great fun. That is until some horses suddenly came up from behind and spooked their donkeys.

MILDRED 'SIS' AND LESTER ROUGEOT
PIONEER DAY PARADE - 1935

"Those donkeys took off runnin'," Lester hooted. Up the street, past the Grange float, Lester and Sis stayed aboard as their stiff legged mounts continued to pound the pavement past the rest of the entrants. Although it wasn't a race it would have been nice if it had been because Lester and Sis crossed the finish line before everyone else in the parade.

Pioneer Day's parade was, and still is, an event where bystanders cheer horseback entrants, old wagons, and floats filled with folks from pioneer families, as they rolled down the streets of Paso Robles. Lester was enthusiastic about participating, in part because of his interest in the Grange, which began long before he was thirteen and a half, the minimum age he was allowed to join the juvenile division.

A few years later, Lester was old enough to be an official member of the Grange. At the time, Dovie Freeman, Lester's grandmother, was an officer. Naturally she would have appreciated it if her grandson had been a disciplined and well-behaved participant in Grange meetings. But that would have been asking a lot from someone who, quite possibly from birth, has been impulsive and fun-loving character.

It was during one meeting, when Lester was caught rolling grapes across the floor, to a friend on the opposite side of the room, that there were two disapproving women who made a fuss about his behavior. Lester's grandmother was not one to bear the burden of a tarnished reputation for long. Dovie knew when Lester turned seventeen her grandson would be eligible for nomination as an officer. Sure enough, when the time came, she nominated him. He was voted in, as Marshall, and subsequently assigned very adult duties within the Grange. Surprising as it was to some, he handled his responsibilities with admirable proficiency and professionalism.

Gratification and pride magnified Dovie's smile when Lester proved to be competent at his first elected position. Dovie enjoyed asking, "What do ya think of my grandson now?" as she shot an 'I told you so' look at two particular doubters.

"It was Ruby Alberti ," Lester recalled. "She said, 'We didn't think he could do it 'cause he's always screwin' around'."

But Lester did do it back in the early 1940's, and quite well. Seventy-plus years later, in 2012, he continues to act as an officer, Master of the El Paso de Robles Grange #555.

"My grandparents, Rega and Dovie Freeman, started the first Grange in the area," Lester asserted. "Grange Halls around the country were constructed and organized as ag fraternities. One thing, we never talk religion or politics. We discuss current concerns for farmers and fund raising events, ways we can make things better for the kids. We have 4-H chapters that meet here at the Paso Robles Grange. And we don't charge 'em."

That's not to say the Grange Hall couldn't use some money for improvements. They could. Old structures have needs - especially when they're in California's earthquake country.

"My grandparents were very involved in the Grange. Went to the meetings, the California State Conventions, they helped a lot of people." Lester leaned forward and rested his arms on the long table inside the dining area at the El Paso de Robles Grange Hall. Deserted and quiet, that day, the place felt more like a granddad's hunting cabin than a formal meeting hall. Modest in décor the old building appeared to be rustic but in fairly good condition, thanks to Lester and his crew of volunteers.

No elaborate, pretentious, or expensive furnishings - just the basics - the necessities used to put on a feast and provide shelter, and that's it. Kitchen rafters exposed, kitchen cabinets plain, appliances mismatched, yet the simplicity of it all made the place feel hospitable and useful. A hub of activity since 1946 the building has been well used.

Next to the steps that lead up to the kitchen door, set in a planting area surrounded with flowers, a natural stone pillar harvested from a farm field especially for Lester's wife, Barbara Hatch Rougeot's memorial plaque, adorns the side of the barbeque area which overlooks rolling hills and dales to the south. Barbara, an active participant and contributor to Grange ambitions, was always there to lend a most helpful hand. Lester took it upon himself to give his wife an official shout-out, applause, recognition, and thanks, by erecting a stately monument in honor of the woman who, for more than six decades, had donated her organizational skills, her wisdom, and her moral support to whatever causes the Grange and Lester were involved in.

BARBARA ROUGEOT'S MEMORIAL
EL PASO DE ROBLES GRANGE #555

"The Grange started when people wanted to oppose the price of shipping," Lester said. "People got together to fight the railroad. The heyday for the Grange was during the depression. Back in the thirties people needed each other."

Mutual concern over agriculturally related issues persuaded people of the Monterey and San Luis Obispo Counties to get onboard, to take united stands as others in the nation had done beginning in 1867, and the state of California in 1873. When, in 1932, at an existing rural community center that had been constructed in 1915, Lester's grandparents, Rega Dent Freeman and his wife, Dovie Nicklas Freeman, founded the first Grange in the area, known as the Estrella Grange #488, it was the beginning of a family tradition. Decades later in 2012, family members including Lester, his daughter, Regina, and his son, Chester, continue to occupy themselves with Grange goals and activities.

Grange's ceremonial splendor and parliamentary procedures keep the group's focus on a high level of standards. Though their practices may seem outdated to some they still appear to serve a purpose, as in they build character, develop leadership, and promote cooperation.

When it comes to the hierarchy of the group, the Grange has been historically known for their promotion of positions of power choosing the person rather than the person choosing the position of power. They recognize that people often have conflicting and opposing opinions, which is not morally wrong as it often encourages advancement of truth, especially when contrary individuals can agree to disagree rather than waste time quarreling.

Being a champion for community and family betterment, the Grange is the country's organization that sponsored 4-H clubs, Boy and Girl Scouts, Campfire girls, Future Farmers of America, and fairs – all groups that bring people together. They organized insurance co-ops and sponsored credit unions. In 1937, the Estrella Grange launched the first federal credit union in San Luis Obispo County and it was Rega and Dovie Freeman who were instrumental in the accomplishment of that ambition.

"My grandparents started the First Federal Grange Credit Union in the area," Lester said as he straightened and expanded. A charter member of a Grangers Credit Union, Lester would later be its President.

Evidence shows, with a lineage of go-getters, trailblazers who preceded him, Lester came by his leadership abilities and his passion for undertaking and directing projects quite honestly, maybe even genetically. What Lester learned from his family, by example and by encouragement, was how to contribute by way of being a productive member of society. By being involved, for the past three quarters of a century, in Grange meetings, agendas, and activities, as well as countless other irons he has in fires all over the county, Lester did, and does, just that.

Practiced at official Grange duties, and proficient at all things ranch and farm related, Lester also gained practical and social skills, not to mention knowledge, when he was in the Paso Robles High School's Future Farmers of America, F.F.A. which he, yet again, credits his grandparents and the Grange for making possible both the program and the competitions.

"My grandparents, Rega and Dovie Freeman, were interested and involved in the F.F.A. and the local fair," Lester announced. "Being avid Grangers, they, along with another Grange Member, Ruby Alberti, from San Luis Obispo Grange, made a motor trip to Sacramento, to the State Grange Office, to get seed money for the San Luis Obispo Fair. You know, there was a lot of discussion whether twenty-six thousand or twenty-seven thousand dollars was too much money to spend on the property where the Mid State Fair now sits." Lester laughed.

It was 1941when Rega and Dovie Freeman and Ruby Alberti managed to persuade the California State Grange to fund the first San Luis Obispo County fair. Lester's grandmother, Dovie, served on the fair's first board of trustees, and in February of 2006, both she and Lester's grandfather, Rega, were inducted, posthumously, into the Mid State Fair's Hall of Fame. That same day Lester and his wife, Barbara, were formally installed as Hall of Famers as well. Honored with a ceremony and awarded with a bronzed long-horned steer sculpture it was acknowledgment of their great efforts over the many years.

"So, in 1941 and 1942, Paso had this fair across from where Robbins Field is now," Lester recalled. Robbins Field is located between Sixth and Seventh Streets and Pine and Park Streets. The fair was originally known as the San Luis Obispo County 16th District Agricultural Fair. "We'd set up pens in the vacant lot. Only two of us showed steers. Kenny Kester from Shandon had Angus and took all the awards in that class. I showed Herefords and took all of the awards in that class. Years later it was brought to our attention that my wife, Barbara's, great grandparents, the Lamberts, had actually owned part of the land where the fairgrounds are, to the South."

LESTER ROUGEOT

Although at Grange benefits Lester has been known to be in front of the grill flipping pancakes and behind the barbeque pit timing tri tips of beef, chicken, and his famous garlic bread sans garlic - a little trick of Lester's to put the garlic in the fire rather than slather it on the sourdough - his son, Chester, claimed Lester's specialty is that of a one man entertainment committee.

"Dad works the room and keeps everyone laughing."

"That seasoning that I use they're callin', 'Lester Dust'," Lester said. "It's Dick Waer's recipe. People just love it." Dick Waer's secret blend of herbs and spices, also known as Lester Dust, was so dubbed by Ed Hale's son, John Hale.

According to an article in the 2012 Spring Issue of the California Grange News written by State Master Bob McFarland, eating some of Lester's dusted tri-tips of beef is so pleasing to the palate it's like being, "on a second honeymoon".

"So tasty is Lester's BBQ that he's got "groupies" that follow him around town," Bob McFarland wrote. "It's not unusual to see Lester lounging around at a local restaurant with one or two of these lovely ladies seated at his table! Begging the question, 'What does this eighty-six year old Grange cowboy got that I ain't?' I don't visit Lester much. He gives me an inferiority complex."

BARBARA AND LESTER ROUGEOT WITH EMILY FREEMAN.
PHYLISS WILKINSON, JOHNNY AND GLADYS CRASPAY

Uproarious laughter came from the middle of the room where Lester stood visiting with people who had come for the pancake breakfast. A table full of smiling people interacted with him as 4-H members scurried with plates full of appetizing fare. The atmosphere was more than hospitable, it was jovial. The event seemed to bring people together in a way that made friendship effortless and uncomplicated.

The crew of regular volunteers worked like a synchronized orchestra at the monthly Grange pancake breakfast. The tap, clink, and whir of kitchen activity along with the happy chatter of the people and the aroma of hotcakes, bacon, and coffee, oh yeah, very contented atmosphere as the helpers hustled to serve more than six dozen breakfasts every second Sunday of every month.

Chester Rougeot had arrived at the Grange around four-thirty in the morning to fire up the ovens and bake the bacon. Bacon which Lester repeatedly bragged had been donated by Joe Ontiveros of Joe's Places in Paso Robles and Templeton. Kept warm and at the ready an abundance of bacon to his side, Chester flipped flapjacks at the grill, Ed Hale scrambled and cooked eggs, John Camino washed dishes, Pat Hippensteel kept the coffee brewed and the paper shot glasses of orange juice filled, Blanche Camino took the money at the front desk, 4-H Leaders supervised the 4-H workers.

"Ya know, to get all this done you have a lot of help. Ed Hale, he cooks the eggs and he's the Paso Robles Grange Treasurer. I couldn't have done it without Ed," Lester said. "You couldn't ask for more honest treasurer than Ed," Lester said then laughed. "If Ed loses a penny he's spend two days lookin' for it."

Month after month, year after year some of the same people continued to offer their time at these events. Walk into the room or the barbeque area and most of the faces were familiar with the exception of that guy with the red beard. His green hat and green vest, embellished with four leaf clovers, were very stylish on Saint Patrick's Day. Who is that guy? It's the same guy who, the following month, contorted his torso and wiggled into a one-piece white Easter bunny suit, topped with big upright ears and little whiskers. Why? For the same reason he wore a dress on Mother's day and a Santa suit for Christmas - to put a smile on people's faces. All in the name of fun – and it is – for everyone.

Lester's eldest daughter, Regina, a professional seamstress, custom made Lester's seasonal costumes. She has encouraged and supported Lester's antics.

CHESTER ROUGEOT, JOHN CAMINO, LESTER ROUGEOT, TONY MACERA, ED HALE

Left - LESTER ROUGEOT AS THE EASTER BUNNY
Right - JERRY ASHTON WITH HIS MOTHER'S DAY DATE, LESTER ROUGEOT

LESTER ROUGEOT
GRANGE CONVENTION 1986

SANTA AT ADA'S VINEYARD

BREAKFASTS AND BARBEQUES
- ❖ Heritage Oaks Fun Run Pancake breakfast in November
- ❖ Mid-State Fair's free pancake breakfast - feeds 1600+ people in 3 hours
- ❖ Farm Supply Customer Appreciation BBQ - feeds 700-800 people
- ❖ Birthday parties
- ❖ Graduations
- ❖ Weddings
- ❖ Brandings
- ❖ Memorial services
- ❖ Paso Robles Library Volunteers BBQ
  and the list goes on...

Lester's crew works the barbeques or breakfast on a volunteer/donation basis. "They treat us good," Lester commented on how the organizations or individuals they have cooked for often donate money to the 7X Ranch/Campground. 4-H members lend a hand at many of these functions in order to earn points that help them advance within the organization. It's a win-win system all the way around thanks to the generosity of people, like Lester and crew, who are willing to give of their time and energy in service of their community.

LESTER ROUGEOT BARBEQUES TRI TIPS OF BEEF
FARM SUPPLY CUSTOMER APPRECIATION BARBEQUE

ORGANIZATIONS
- ❖ Greenriver Water Company – President
- ❖ Native Sons of Golden West San Miguel Parlor 150 - Charter Member (Lester is the only Charter Member left), President, Treasurer, Life Member
- ❖ Estrella Grange #488 – member since 1939
- ❖ El Paso de Robles Grange #555 – Master
- ❖ Grangers Credit Union – Charter Member, President
- ❖ Pomona Grange #27 San Luis Obispo County – President since 1975
- ❖ California State Grange – State Deputy
- ❖ National Grange – Member
- ❖ Paso Robles High School F.F.A. - Charter Member, Life Member, State Degree
- ❖ Friends of the Adobe - President, Vice President
- ❖ North County Council on Youth – President
- ❖ Cuesta Chapter Credit Union – President
- ❖ Senior Citizens Community Support – Member
- ❖ Honorary Member Kiwanis
- ❖ Father Reginald Park - San Miguel
- ❖ 7X Ranch – 1992 - 2008 Trustee

AWARDS
- ❖ White Stetson – Davies Ranch Fire
- ❖ Honorary Chapter Farmer - Paso Robles F.F.A. 1966
- ❖ Master Salesman for GMC – 1977
- ❖ Friends of 4-H Award for San Luis Obispo County – 1992
- ❖ Roblan of the Month – 1993
- ❖ Sage Brush Days – Marshall
- ❖ Fair Blue Ribbon Award
- ❖ Main Street Award
- ❖ Mid State Fair Pancake Breakfast Organizer
- ❖ Mid State Fair Blue Ribbon Award – 1994
- ❖ Ranchita 4-H Appreciation Award
- ❖ National Council of Alcohol and Drug Dependency
- ❖ Roblan of the Year - 2002
- ❖ Heritage Oaks Fun Run – 2001

- ❖ Mid State Fair Hall of Fame – 2006
- ❖ Pioneer Day Marshall – 2007
- ❖ Granger of the year – 2011
- ❖ The Exchange Club – The Book of Golden Deeds Award 2012
- ❖ Friends of the Adobe – 2012.

LESTER ROUGEOT ROBLAN OF THE MONTH APRIL 1993

At the 2002 Roblan of the Year ceremony, Ed Hale acted as Lester presenter.

"Ed Hale, he's been a damn good friend," Lester blurted.

BARBARA ROUGEOT LOOKS ON AS LESTER IS AWARDED
ROBLAN OF THE YEAR - 2002

As additional acknowledgement for his Roblan of the Year Award, Lester received certificates from Senator Bruce McPherson from the 15th Senatorial District, Congressman Bill Thomas, and Assemblyman Abel Maldonado from the 33rd Assembly District – all in recognition of his, "outstanding, exemplary, and dedicated service".

When Lester was elected Marshall of Paso Robles' Pioneer Day in 2007, his childhood switch swinging babysitter, Ruth Quenser, sent him a card which read in part, "I never thought that little kid in the tree would ever become Pioneer Day Marshall." That card meant a lot to Lester.

Eighty-two year old Marshall Lester Rougeot presented the Pioneer Day Queen and her attendants with fans, and all the Belles with red roses. He attended all the Pioneer Day functions accompanied by wife Barbara. During the actual parade, much like Marshall Matt Dillon, in the old television show, Gunsmoke, Lester sat tall atop a big buckskin horse, with nephew, Roger Miller, and son, Chester Rougeot to his sides, as his outriders. Daughter, Regina Rougeot Bonds and cousin, Kay Nicklas drove Lester's 1953 CJ3B Willies Jeep behind them with a mounting block in the back of the jeep for Lester.

"My brother, Roger, furnished the horses and tack for Uncle Lester and Chester for the Pioneer Day parade when Uncle Lester was Marshall," Judy Miller said and added the saddles were contestant saddles that Roger had won for his roping skills.

ROUGEOT/HATCH PIONEER FAMILY WINDOW DISPLAY BY REGINA ROUGEOT BONDS

LESTER ROUGEOT
PIONEER DAY MARSHALL – 2007

MARSHALL LESTER ROUGEOT
FLANKED BY ROGER MILLER AND CHESTER ROUGEOT
PIONEER DAY – 2007

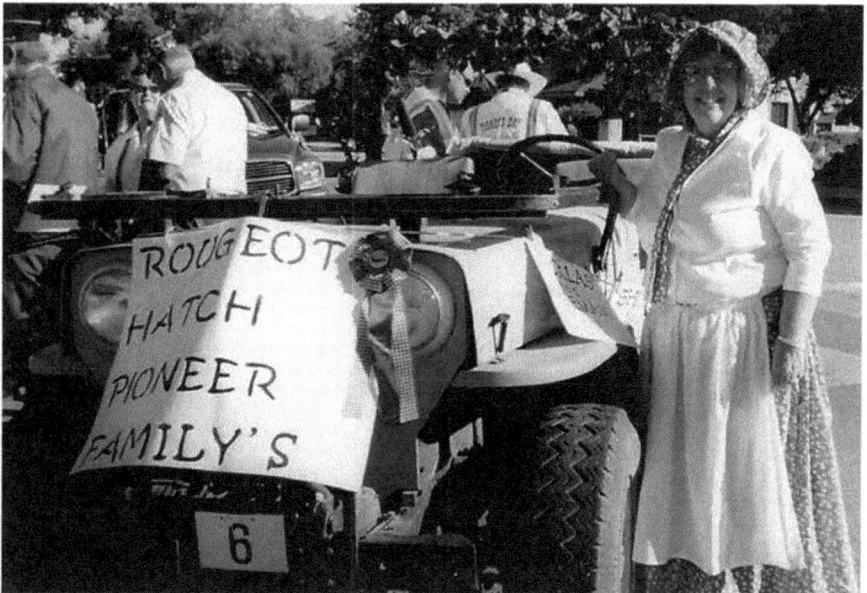

REGINA ROUGEOT BONDS WITH CJ3B WILLIES JEEP
PIONEER DAY PARADE – 2007

BARBARA AND LESTER ROUGEOT
MID STATE FAIR HALL OF FAME INDUCTION - 2006

LESTER ROUGEOT GRANGER OF THE YEAR – 2011

FRIENDS OF THE ADOBE AWARD
2012

In addition to Lester being the 2007 Pioneer Day Marshall, Lester's mother, Thelma Rougeot was the 1983 Pioneer Day Queen, as was Lester's sister, Gladys in 2006.

There's a house full of awards, plaques, and newspaper articles hanging on walls, propped against the couch, on the kitchen and coffee tables, in corners and drawers, and who knows where else. Lester the Marshall of Paso Robles Pioneer Day, Lester the Roblan of the Year, Barbara and Lester being inducted into the Hall of Fame, Barbara's bowling trophies, Lester's blue ribbons, multiple Paso Robles Press clippings, and on and on. Lester's mug shot has been in the paper many times – and thankfully for reasons that make his family proud. Besides all the interviews Lester granted to the talented staff at the Paso Robles Press he has been interviewed on live radio by Dick Mason, Paso Robles' KPRL radio station personality from which Lester has CD recordings to enjoy.

The best thing – if a house is going to be cluttered with something – what better than visual validation of the appreciation they received for their countless hours of volunteer time?

At a table inside Joe's Place in Templeton Lester's blue eyes twinkled. He pulled a wooden plaque from a black drawstring bag

"Look what they gave me," he said. "I had no idea they was doin' this for me. I thought I was there to talk about the 7X." Lester expression was one of humbled surprise as he held up The Book of Golden Deeds Award from the Exchange Club. After showing it off to interested people who passed the table he carefully put it back in its protective fabric bag then laughed.

"My daughter, Regina, says I've got so damn many of these things she says she's gonna have my coffin made out of 'em."

9 – FOUNTAINS FOR YOUTH

To turn thoughts into action was, and still is, something Lester Rougeot excelled at, especially when his ideas involved child-like fun. His vision for a near triangular-shaped piece of property, just yards away from Mission San Miguel, was no exception.

"After a San Miguel Parlor Native Sons meeting one night I wondered, 'Why doesn't somebody do somethin' with this ground'," Lester said. He had driven by the parcel of open land many times. It seemed a waste to Lester. At that time the space didn't look like much more than a patch of weeds. However, to Lester, it had the potential to be usable.

Although others had similar thoughts about the space it would take someone like Lester, someone who sees possibilities, not obstacles, to take charge.

"I talked it over with Barb and we made a plan. I asked Gene Machado to find out who owned the property and he found out it was the County."

Though others had envisioned the land as a possible park, and there was already a stone pillar monument on the west side of the plot, in honor of Colonel John C. Fremont, no one had managed to secure official authorization to do so, until Lester.

"Colonel Fremont and his soldiers camped on a nearby hill," Lester informed. "The monument is for him.

Lester contacted the County of San Luis Obispo. He made phone calls, he knocked on government doors, and he pounded the pavement until he found a County agent who not only listened but agreed to meet with him. They talked over ideas and soon Lester had an encroachment permit, in his name, to start work on a park.

As anyone who has ever dealt with the county, or any government agency, knows there was undoubtedly more effort involved than Lester humbly makes known. But when he told the story he gave the impression that without much trouble, he was given permission to do what he had proposed.

What Lester had planned, for the vacant ground surrounding the Fremont monument, was a park complete with grass, trees, picnic tables, benches, a water fountain, and a safety fence. A cement walkway leading to the monument and a fire hydrant would also be on the list of projects to complete.

Lester not only had an action plan for the park, he had recruited help to proceed with the project. The day of the ground breaking, March 13, 1993, was quite a sight, one that caused people to take their eyes off the road as they drove by. It wasn't tractors or gas fueled tillers that were used to turn the wild grasses under and work the soil. Instead, hardworking volunteers did it the old fashioned way – with horses that pulled a plow.

GROUND BREAKING AT FATHER REGINALD MEMORIAL PARK WITH JULES DELWICHE'S BELGIUM HORSES

"Jules Delwiche brought in his team of Belgium horses," Lester boasted. "We did the ground breaking with those horses."

FATHER REGINALD MEMORIAL PARK
GROUND BREAKING

Once the area was down to bare dirt, out came the shovels. Where a backhoe would have scooped out holes for trees in a matter of minutes volunteers used manpower instead. They plunged their shovels into the earth and dug holes for nine mulberry trees.

FATHER REGINALD MEMORIAL PARK
SAN MIGUEL MISSION IN BACKGROUND

LESTER ROUGEOT AND GENE MACHADO
FATHER REGINALD MEMORIAL PARK

"John Wolf built the fence around the park. He welded the pipe together for the fence and all that. One guy started it and had a heart attack. John finished it."

Families came from near and far who benefited from Lester's initiative. At one point, during the building of Father Reginald Memorial Park, a fellow volunteer suggested the park be named after Lester. Although Lester had been instrumental in all phases of the park's design, planning, and construction it wasn't done for his personal glory. He did it for the purpose of providing a place where parents could bring their children and watch them play. He did it to better an area sorely lacking in public places for healthy childrens' activities.

As with the many ways in which Lester contributed, and still contributes, he started the park as a community service. Lester insisted the park be named after Father Reginald, a father at Mission San Miguel whom Lester had been friends with until he passed. The park was dedicated on November 4, 1995, to Father Reginald McDonough (April 4, 1911 - August 8, 1988) by the Native Sons of the Golden West Parlor #150.

"Father Reginald," Lester said, "he was a real nice guy."

As if they weren't busy enough, at the same time Lester and Barbara had been working on Father Reginald Memorial Park, the couple had taken on an even bigger project.

"How it all started, someone left this envelope on Virginia Peterson's step," Lester began. "It had these papers in it and she read 'em and didn't know what to do. Monica Bryan told Virginia, 'You get that to Lester', and she did. I read it and said, 'Time's about up."

Evidently an anonymous donor thought time was up too. According to what Lester read, land and money from the Dee and Minnabel Fitzhugh estate, had been put in the hands of a trustee. As directed by the Fitzhughs the trustee was to see to the making of a wilderness campground, for use by supervised children. When Lester was informed that the quarter million dollars left in the trust had rapidly dwindled as pay for trustee and lawyer fees, as well as caretaker wages, that's when he looked into the situation for himself. What he found gave him the determination to see that Fitzhughs' directives for the land be carried out. When Lester saw there had been no benefit for the intended purpose he stepped up to the plate and started swinging. If Dee Fitzhugh had designated the land for the area's youth, then by golly, that's what should happen.

Though the Fitzhughs were unable to have any children of their own, the couple loved young people. That's why they left eighty acres, on Cypress Mountain Road, eighteen miles west of Spring Street in Paso Robles, and enough funds to provide children a peaceful and private location to study the physical world. Which in turn they knew would promote exploration and enhancement of a child's internal landscape as well.

The Fitzhughs knew the value of a wilderness experience. They knew how it felt to dip their toes in the creek, how pleasurable it was to have a picnic in the middle of a meadow, how it aroused emotion to observe a doe lick her fawn, or how empowering it was to survive the elements. They intended and expected the scenic area they had set aside for a campground to be enjoyed by youth groups from all local walks of life. It was their gift to the youth, their contribution to humanity. After all, what better thing is there to give the world, than a child who appreciates life?

"The money had about run out," Lester informed.

If action wasn't taken immediately the funds, designated to pay for expenses incurred during the building of the campground, would be gone. When Lester said, "Time's about up, we gotta do somethin' here," he wasn't kidding.

"Most the money went to the trustee. Highest paid one year was twenty-four thousand dollars plus two thousand dollars a month to his son to live there," Lester said.

Dollars meant to develop the camp had dwindled away with no sign of progress, whatsoever.

"Then I went out there and talked to the attorney for three hours," Lester continued.

For seven years there had been no development according to the Fitzhughs' wishes. Pressure to resign was placed on the trustee by concerned citizens so when Lester started pitching his plan that's when the assigned trustee rapidly struck out, called it a game, and handed Lester the bat. The new trustee, Lester Rougeot, took over in late 1992. But not before the heirs contested the will, and in the process, allegedly lost hundreds of thousands of dollars in legal costs.

"So I decided to take this thing on as a Grange project," Lester said. "Formed the North County Council for Youth, registered it with the state, all in my name as a non-profit organization."

No fly by night operation there. Lester made sure everything was on the up and up. He arranged a North County Council for Youth meeting, elected officers, made it all official.

"We did it like we were supposed to but it never panned out like it was supposed to because they had a board of directors," Lester said. "I was elected president of it then appointed someone from each youth group to be on the board. Girl Scouts, Boy Scouts, 4-H. Only once did they come out and do anything." Lester's eyes cast to the floor he shook his hat covered head. A deep sigh told of his disappointment. After all the time he'd spent in preparation of giving these groups a voice; a chance to participate in a most worthy cause, it disheartened Lester that people just couldn't find the time to get involved.

"Somebody said, 'Who's your board of directors', I said, 'Hell I don't have a board of directors'," Lester recalled, "'I took care of it myself. Now, I don't have to screw with 'em'." He pushed his hat down tighter on his head; a subconscious indication of his determination.

"When I got home the attorney calls me and says, 'I'd like to come out again tomorrow. I got somethin' I want to tell you.' That's when he nominated, appointed me the trustee. He says to me, 'You're the only person who wants to make a campground and not line your pockets'."

That was true. The only money Lester took during his time as trustee of the 7X Ranch was twenty-six hundred dollars for expenses. He never took a trustee fee or even money for mileage. A pay check was not his motivation. Lester took on the 7X Campground project because he was sure it was the right thing to do. He and his wife, Barbara knew it would benefit local children. Those motivations encouraged them to muster enough dedication to march through muddles of red tape. It was their fortitude that made them forge onward through unfriendly territory. As with everything else in Lester's life, it was his internal compass, that guidance system that was installed long ago, that drove him to see the 7X project to completion.

Though Lester had been disappointed by the initial lack of participation, particularly in regards to the North County Council for Youth, his disappointment didn't last long. The purity of Lester's intentions ended up attracting many good people who showed up to help with everything from their scrub brushes to backhoes.

In the later part of 1992, the 7X began to get the once over. From top to bottom the place was transformed from a rundown ranch to a cared for camp.

"Bob Healey loaned us a backhoe," Lester said," for the whole time. And Roho Construction sent out a backhoe to use too."

Trenches were dug for water lines, roads were graded and graveled, campsites were leveled and plumbed with fire hydrants and drinking water, regulation bathrooms complete with flushing toilets and showers were constructed.

"Tony Macera built the bathrooms," Lester credits. "Showers, flush toilets, and the septic system, it was all volunteers."

Naturally a big clean up and construction project required a large amount of trash be hauled away.

"Dale Gomer's family, they've had Paso Robles Garbage for more than fifty years. They brought out a twenty yard bin and told us to call 'em when it was full. They emptied that thing for free and they still come out and don't charge anything." Lester laughed. "Gomer says, 'Lester, you're hard to turn down'."

TYPICAL DIG AT THE 7X RANCH

During the construction phase of the project many good folks donated their time.

"The Paso Robles Lyons Club helped us out," Lester mentioned. "And the Paso Robles Water Department, by God, those guys put in the water system, the water lines and fire hydrants and drinking water. We were required to put in fire hydrants at every site." Water for the 7X Campground comes from a mountain spring. There is also a back-up well.

"We get the water tested," Lester mentioned. "It's pure spring water."

As trustee, Lester supervised the building of the 7X youth camp as did Keith Rhyne, Lester's distant cousin, who was the first manager Lester hired.

"Keith's a retired Coronel from the Air Force," Lester shared. "He and his wife, Jaci, did a lot of work out there."

As did Skip Dodd. "Skip, he did everything he could for me," Lester praised. Skip operated heavy equipment to dig trenches in land that was notoriously rocky. His wife, Nancy, scrubbed and cleaned.

The caretaker's house needed attention as well as the area set aside for camping. Hardwood floors inside the main ranch house were refinished. The chimney was repaired. "That guy come out there and fixed that chimney for free," Lester marveled. "Wouldn't accept pay."

CHIMNEY REPAIR AT THE 7X RANCH

BACKHOE OPERATOR – KEITH RHYNE
7X RANCH

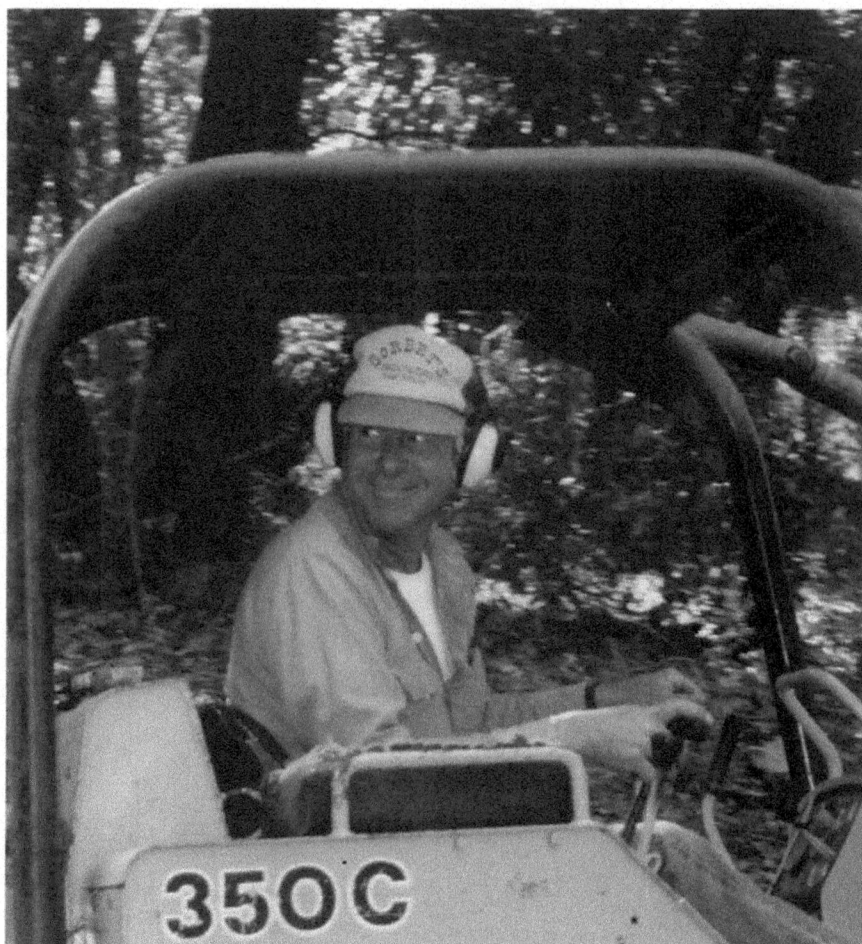

GENE GORBETT – BULLDOZER OPERATOR
7X CAMPGROUND CONSTRUCTION

In fact, there were many folks who wouldn't take money. Though there were costs involved in the making of the 7X Campground, the bighearted people who came to contribute to the cause, did so for reasons other than their bank accounts.

"Gene Gorbett worked out there," Lester said. "He brought out a little dozer. I tried to pay 'im and when I asked, 'What do I owe ya?', he said, 'You don't owe me nothin'.' I says, 'Aw, you gotta let me pay ya somethin'. At least let me pay for your fuel. Gene says, 'Lester, if you pay me I'm never comin' back'."

196

KEITH RHYNE REFINISHES FLOOR
7X RANCH HOUSE

GENE GORBETT AND SKIP DODD

DICK AVERY

Generous people around the community thundered out the scenic narrow road to help.

"Ole Viborg helped us out and his son, Paul Viborg, brought out equipment and base material, BG they call it, for the roads and stuff."

The project proceeded and before long the 7X was a functional campground. Five hillside campsites with picnic tables nestled under the shade of old oaks had been cleared of brush and poison oak. Tent sites had been leveled for comfort.

While the caretakers and hosts encourage the majority of their guests time be spent in the great outdoors, there are also indoor activities, such as ping pong.

"Jules Delwiche donated a pool table and overhead light," Lester added.

Near the 7X Ranch's original buildings, there are artifacts, a nature trail, corral facilities for occasion overnight horse guests.

"Dee liked Indian bowls," Sue Cinque informed. "So he used to make them. You can tell which ones he made because they're perfect." Sue and her husband, Bruce, are the current caretakers and managers of the 7X. They accepted the position in December of 2002.

Sue also pointed out an available area designated for archery, a portable barbeque, and fire pits as well as a spot for a group campfire - for that primitive tribe-like, back-to-basics bonding experience.

In addition to the campsites, Lester's crew of volunteers created a picnic area. Located along Las Tablas Creek near Minnabel's Meadow, there are tables, benches, a barbeque, and electricity. More regulation bathrooms and drinking water are conveniently located nearby. There, children can play horseshoes, volleyball, or a field sport at the playing field.

"Minnabel Meadow is day use and overnight," Sue stated. "Tent camping, there's only five level sites. We're on a donation basis and groups normally stay two nights."

Both the campground and the picnic areas have access to an emergency telephone.

"In order to enjoy the 7X," Sue said, "children must live in Northern San Luis Obispo County and be under eighteen years old. For every ten children there must be one adult."

LESTER ROUGEOT AT THE PUMP HOUSE
7X RANCH – MINNABEL MEADOW

Reservation can be secured through Bruce or Sue Cinque at 805-238-1500. The Cinques ask guests to sign a release of liability form before they are allowed to make camp.

LESTER ROUGEOT WITH CARL OSCAR BORG PAINTING

KEITH AND JACI RHYNE, LESTER AND BARBARA ROUGEOT
CARL OSCAR BORG PAINTING

All that - the campground, the bathrooms, the picnic area down the road at Minnabel's Meadow, and the repairs made to the caretaker's house - it all had to be accomplished with a meager amount of money left over from years of ineffective expenditures. However, as luck would have it, the 7X had a windfall while under Lester's trusteeship. While he was in charge, Lester discovered a large painting, thought to be left behind by Pete Beronio. The painting was by Carl Oscar Borg, a Swedish American artist and poet (1879-1947) from Dals-Grinstad, Sweden. At one time Borg taught art in Santa Barbara. He was commissioned by Phoebe Apperson Hearst to paint several Native American ceremonies. The large painting that Lester found, in the 7X ranch house, turned out to be of Captain McGuire catching seals, oil on canvas, sixty inches by forty-one inches, signed by Carl Oscar Borg, Santa Cruz, 1908. The painting depicts cowboys roping a seal lion with six men in the foreground, a small boat, and three men in the distance with a small boat.

After having the painting appraised Lester sold it to a Santa Barbara museum. The money was added to the dwindling funds of the Dee Fitzhugh trust.

"We made fifty-five thousand dollars on that painting," Lester recalled with wide eyes.

Thanks are due to Sue Cinque for providing historical information about the 7X Ranch. The eighty acres is at an elevation of twelve to thirteen hundred feet. The description of the property's physical location is: W ½ of NE ¼ of section 8, Township 27S Range 10E Mt Diablo. It was first owned by Albert Johnson.

Albert Johnson sold the quick claim rights to J.W. Bagby in 1906. Bagby was a cattleman who registered the 7X brand in 1889. He used the same brand for two different purposes. Depending on which way the brand was held it was either a 7X, or an XL brand when inverted. The 7X brand differentiated and identified which cattle Bagby owned and the XL brand marked the ones he owed money on, to creditors.

Elizabeth Bagby sold to Charles C. Thompson in 1928. Thompson, a world hunter, improved the ranch house, built a wild game trophy room, the greenhouse, trails, and stonework.

Thompson sold to Pierre C. Merillon in 1943.

Merillon sold to Pete Beronio in 1945. Beronio is believed to be the man who left the Carl Oscar Borg painting behind. He owned the 7X for two months and sold to Frank and Grace Dickey in 1945.

The Dickey's sold to Dee and Minnabel Fitzhugh in 1948. The Fitzhughs had previously lived near Cambria. In the late 1970's the Fitzhughs sold most of the ranch. In 1986 when Dee died he left his estate, including ranch buildings, to the children of north San Luis Obispo County. The ranch was placed in a trust under the management of Jim Ashe for the purpose of establishing a camp and picnic area, which didn't begin to manifest until the torch was passed to Lester in 1992.

By 1994, the 7X had its grand opening celebration. Thanks to Lester and friends, within the first eight months more than six hundred children came and benefited from their wilderness experience. And that was reward enough to Lester, who had invested much of himself into the making of the 7X, as did his wife, Barbara.

Sadly, it all became too much when Barbara began to have health issues in 2006. That's when the couple decided it was time for Lester to turn over the position of trustee to another man. Not just anyone would do, either. It had to be someone of equal integrity, someone knowledgeable about the area, someone with enough gumption to carry on in the interest of the area's youth. That man was Skip Dodd. To this day, July 20, 2012, Skip is the trustee of the 7X.

When Lester thought back on the project, he was humbled by the generosity of his fellow community members. So much so that words lodged in his throat as he managed to say, "And all it cost me was a barbeque."

7X CAMPGROUND

LESTER ROUGEOT AND FRIEND – 7X RANCH

LESTER ROUGEOT WITH JACI AND KEITH RHYNE

CHESTER ROUGEOT, LESTER ROUGEOT, NANCY DODD,
SUE CINQUE, SKIP DODD, AND BRUCE CINQUE – 2012

7X RANCH HOUSE – 2012

RAISING THE FLAG AT 7X RANCH
GRAND OPENING

MINNABEL AND DEE FITZHUGH
7X RANCH

10 – THE COWGIRL RIDES AWAY

At Lester and Barbara's sixtieth anniversary party, life as Lester knew it was about to change. Barbara, who had always been there to help Lester mark calves, drive the tractor, raise their children, and accompany him   nearly everywhere he went, made an announcement at that celebration.

"I've taken care of Lester for sixty years," she said. "Now it's his turn to take care of me."

"Mom was sick the last four years of her life," first born daughter Regina said. "What Mom went through was pretty rough at times. There were good times, her trips with Dad to Joe's for breakfast every morning. Where ever Dad went she went too. Dad stuck by her the whole time. If she was in the hospital or rehab center Dad visited every day, except a couple of times he was sick. Mom was a pretty private person and it was really rough on her, and everyone, during that time."

"Even when Auntie Barbara was at Ada's, we brought her either to her house or mine for Christmas," Judy Miller said. "I believe it was 2009, that my brother, Roger and his sons, Clint and Colt, decided to have us at Roger's house and they did a redneck Christmas tree. They cut it down on the ranch and decorated it with empty shell casings and Copenhagen can lids and beer cans, rope. Of course Auntie Barbara and Uncle Lester thought it was great.

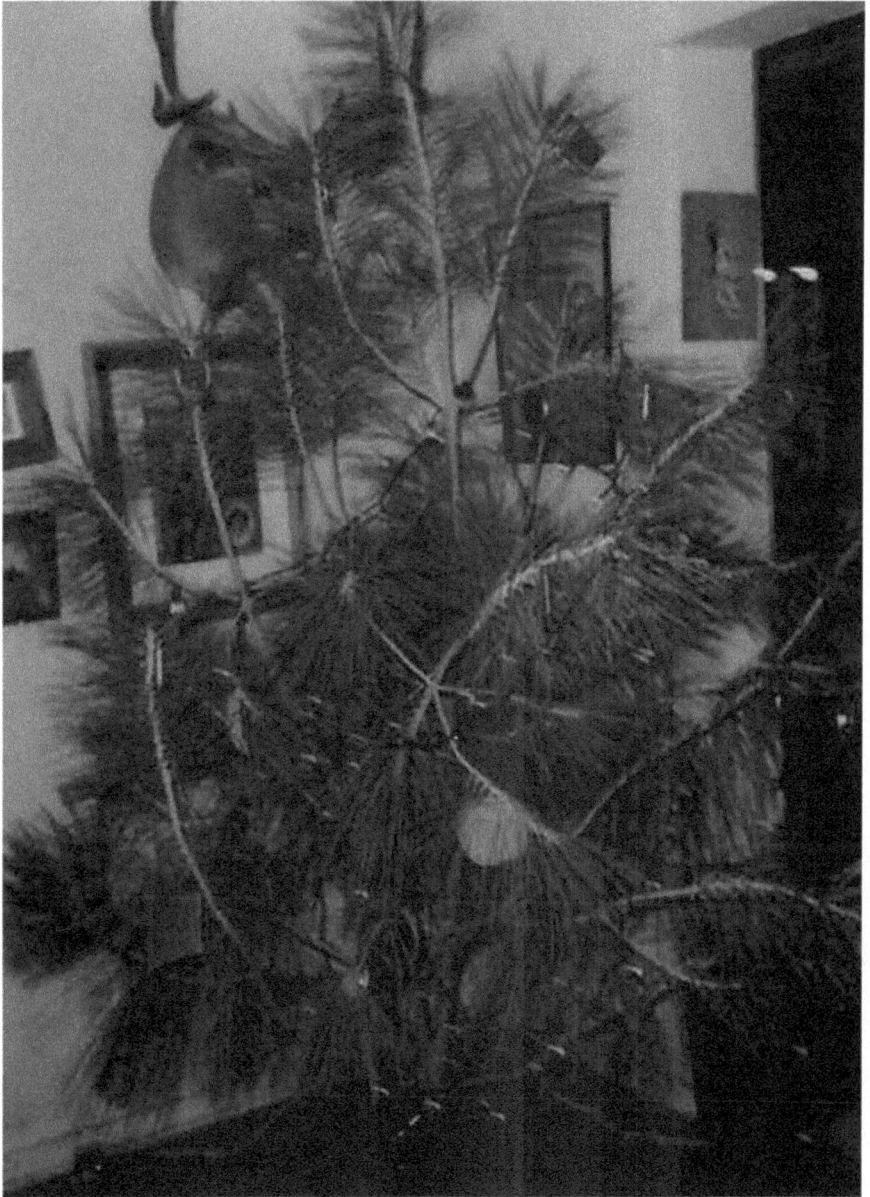

REDNECK CHRISTMAS TREE
DECORATED BY CLINT AND COLT MILLER
FOR THEIR GREAT AUNTIE BARBARA
AND GREAT UNCLE LESTER

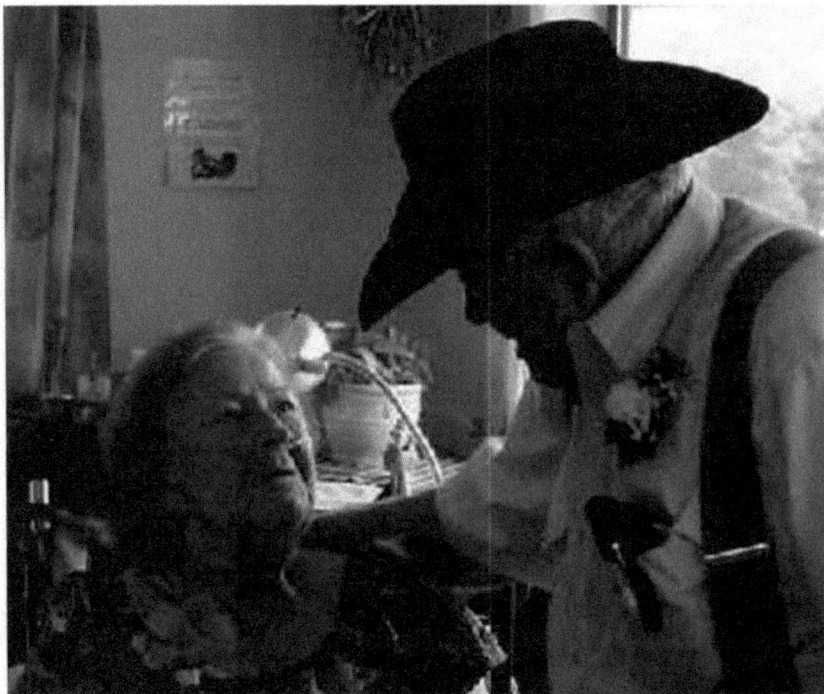

BARBARA AND LESTER ROUGEOT
60TH ANNIVERSARY - APRIL 9, 2006

"Roger and I were the lucky kids, we were the youngest kids of my parents and Auntie and Uncle's kids were grown and moved away, so Roger and I got to do really special things with them, such as deer hunting, jeep riding, and quality togetherness. Auntie Barbara loved little kids and had a tolerance for tricks and games. She may have instigated many of our tricks.

"I know my brother was so happy that Uncle Lester and Auntie Barbara were substitute grandparents to Roger's children, since our parents were deceased. Roger's kids always knew Great Uncle and Great Auntie would be there for all the momentous occasions such as holidays, graduations, and even drove to Parkfield plays."

Barbara's final days were spent in a room at a care facility called Ada's Vineyard. There at the north end of Paso Robles, Lester had reserved a specific room for Barbara, one that looked west across Highway 101, at land where her father had been raised.

"They weren't quite finished with the room I wanted for Barb, so I put a deposit on it so they'd keep it for her. See, there at Ada's she had her own private room and private bath," Lester described. "And there was this barn that was her grandfather's, and was over a hundred years old and she could look and see that barn." It was a meaningful view intended to comfort Barbara.

"I work where Lester's dear wife, Barbara lived her last year or so," Christina Beyler said. "Barb... oh my, she made me laugh everyday with her cowgirl wit."

"Auntie Barbara called it like she saw it," Judy mentioned. "She called the shots as she saw 'em and was always fair, always stuck up for the underdog and even put Uncle Lester in his place when he took teasing too far, calling someone a name, and she'd tell him to look in the mirror."

Christina then revealed, "Lester dressed up as Santa and gave everyone stockings full of goodies around Ada's the past two years. He also dressed up as the Easter Bunny last year as well as he volunteers to put on barbeques for Ada's Alzheimer's Benefit.

"Every year people compliment the wonderful job he does. He is such a caring human being. He always comes in and says 'hi,' to us and always has a smile and a laugh. We could set our clock by Lester," Christina maintained. "We knew in the morning he would go to Joe's and then stop by to see Barb before her breakfast was even over. He would sit next to her at the table and have a cup of coffee and chat with her and the ladies.

"The thing that I remember the most about Lester and Barb," Christina continued, "is they always seemed to laugh." Though she remembered Barbara had a stubborn/independent streak, Christina was quick to mention, "Lester always knew what to do to break down that wall. He loved her so much. And you could just see it in her eyes the way they lit up when she saw him come in."

Times were tough and the situation was sad for all concerned.

"Barb was really somethin'," Lester marveled. Proud eyes moistened and hazed as he bowed his head before the tears spilled. "My God, why couldn't she have stayed longer with me?"

Terminal lung cancer had taken its toll and on July 4, 2010, sixty-four years to the day after giving birth July 4, 1947, to her first born, daughter Regina, Barbara, the country girl who had hammered nails with her dad, wrestled calves for her husband, transported three children to countless activities, and contributed to numerous causes – cast aside the pain, saddled up and rode away.

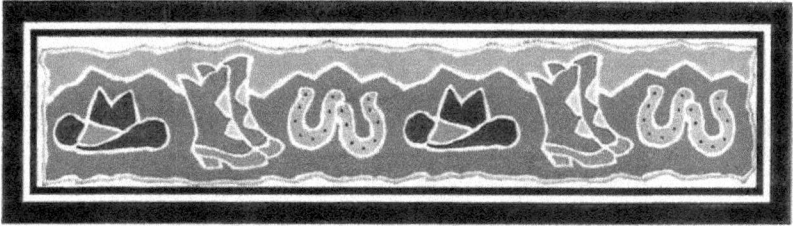

A COWGIRLS LAST REQUEST

Let me tell you folks who have gathered here today,

That I'm a proud and thankful cowgirl who has just passed away.

I know it's hard, but please don't cry,

For I'm now riding Gods trails high up in the sky.

The hoss I'm ridin' now don't spook, buck or kick,

For God stables perfect horses and now I have my pick.

Lord, please forgive me of all my sins,

For I haven't been perfect

But I know that he who believes in you forever wins.

I have lived a good life, a cowgirls dream come true.

Thank you Lord, for now I am ready to ride into eternity

Me, my horse and you.

BARBARA ROUGEOT

1/12/24 – 7/4/10

11 – JOE'S PLACE

The door swung open and Joe's Place, Templeton came alive. Sudden smiles and laughter ensued as Lester sauntered in and greeted the patrons and the employees before he plopped himself into a chair from where he could see everyone who walked in the door.

"I love to hear his cackle in the morning," Mitzi Page said with a contented smile. Mitzi is a server at Lester's favorite breakfast spot. She works at both Joe's Places - the one in Templeton and the one in Paso Robles. To Lester, she's not just a waitress, she's a friend.

"Every morning I start my day off right by comin' to Joe's for breakfast," Lester stated.

As if by magic, a personalized mug appeared full of steaming coffee.

"He has his own coffee mug at both places," Mitzi pointed out.

The people at Joe's Place see Lester so often they have provided him with several of his own customized coffee mugs over the years. Complete with a collage of photographs, one such mug read, "Here comes trouble!" And when that one broke, another one appeared that read, "Here comes trouble's - second mug."

"I've known Lester for five years. I see him every day," Mitzi mentioned. "He knows everybody. When he walks in the door everybody knows him, everybody says hello, everybody talks with him. Every morning, same time, same table. Even if someone's at his table he just sits down with them."

"Barb and I decided we'd go out for breakfast every morning after I retired," Lester recalled. "Every day after that we went out, never had breakfast at home after that."

It was a morning ritual that Lester and Barbara enjoyed together - until she was unable to do so. Sunrise and breakfast with his wife had always been something to look forward to until July 5, 2010.

When Lester opened his eyes that morning, he awoke to the realization that he wouldn't see his wife that day. The woman he had chosen to spend his life with - the one whose clothes hung in the closet and bowling awards embellished the shelves, the one whose energy surrounded him as he looked around the home that had once sheltered their happy family - she had gone to a place where he could no longer look into her eyes and know what she was thinking. Barbara was no longer there to hug as she had been for the previous sixty-four years.

Though his cowgirl had ridden off into the sunset and fireworks, and would suffer no more, it was Lester who would continue to be pained. Flash floods of emotion knocked him to his knees without warning. As if he stood with his back to ocean waves that took him by surprise, uncontrollable anguish over Barbara's absence would wash over him when least expected. Though she'd not slept in their home for nearly a year, their bed had never felt so lonely. Their house had never felt so empty, as Lester forced himself to face his day without her.

With only televised chatter for company, the background noise neither distracted nor masked the deserted living room. Was it an adjustment Lester would ever become comfortable with? Two years later, that remains to be seen.

But Lester wouldn't shut himself away and mourn alone. Wisely, his way to cope with loss was to seek company. And not just any company. It had to be the company of those who cared about him and knew Barbara too. Joe's Places became Lester's home away from home. Joe Ontiveros, his customers, his servers, and kitchen staff all comforted Lester in their own ways. For Lester, Joe's Place was, and still is, a family gathering, emotional support, companionship when he needed it most.

"Barb and I were the first ones in Joe's when he relocated from Twelfth Street to the restaurant where Lolo's was," Lester said. "I was the first one in when Joe opened his restaurant in Templeton too. Did I tell you Joe donates all the bacon for the Grange pancake breakfasts?"

There the kind people, the circle of friends, who surrounded Lester, knew what Barbara and he had been through. They helped Lester survive days without his beloved wife.

"Barbara kept him under control - a little," Mitzi said. "But most of the time she would just let 'im go. She would just shake her head and laugh, except once in awhile she'd say, 'Lester', and he'd straighten right up. Sometimes he'd get himself into trouble and he'd turn to her and say, 'Hey, help me out on this one', and she'd say, 'Oh no, you're on your own'." And now he was - on his own.

Though Barbara would no longer accompany Lester to Joe's there was, and is, comfort in the familiarity there. Lester's routine would remain the same. So much so that he could utter two words, "The usual," and soon his favorite breakfast would be delivered with a smile. A plate full of crispy hash browns, topped with eggs, and a side of raisin toast would go down just fine with that mug of coffee.

"I like my eggs like I like my women," Lester stated. "Flat on their back with their eyes wide open." Mouth agape he roared with laughter at his egg preference portrayal. Eggs that, more commonly, might be called eggs sunny side up.

"You know she won't let me have gravy anymore," Lester said about Mitzi then feigned dejection.

"His doctor told him to lose weight and he's ordering gravy?" Mitzi scoffed. "Give me a break." All the while Mitzi's warm smile and caring gaze lightened the conversation. It was obvious she made Lester's health her concern because of her affection for him. "I was just tellin' Ryan there's been days I switch Lester over to decaf when he gets goin'."

"Oh?" Lester questioned.

"Yeah, when your hat's tipped to the side I know you're up to something and I think, oh no," Mitzi said. "Some days he doesn't get sugar on his French toast either and I tell him, 'You don't need sugar on your French toast'."

"See how they abuse me in here?" Lester asked and laughed.

And still he keeps going back.

"Every little joke that I make, you wouldn't think he'd catch on to," Mitzi began, "and I would hope he wouldn't catch on to, but he does, and then he gets me right back, and he makes me blush just about once a week, and I can't believe that, because it's really hard to make me blush. Like this one time, I used to always snap his suspenders every time he went to leave I'd say, 'Okay, Lester, I'm gonna slingshot you out the door'. I did it for two years and finally one day he just reached around and did it back to me, turned around and he snapped my bra strap." Mitzi gasped and her posture jerked into a straightened and stiffened stance. "I was like, 'Lester!' And it was in a restaurant full of people. He was showin' off. It was so embarrassing but I deserved it."

MITZI PAGE AND LESTER ROUGEOT
AT JOES' PLACE IN TEMPLETON – JUNE 2012

"You know, she offered to take me to the doctor when I told 'er I had an appointment," Lester boasted. "She helped out at the pancake breakfast too, takin' money. And she gave me this."

Lester held up an attractive notebook. Suede looking, masculine – not a frilly flowery two-bit mini paper binder but a nice journal made for a manly man.

"Well, I saw him writin' on the back of his check stub one day and I was like, 'are you serious?' He'd just tear it out and put it his pocket and I'm like, 'you're gonna lose that stuff', so I bought him a little journal."

Mitzi knew Lester had important notes to jot down for the book about his life. Her intuitive and observant awareness of Lester's needs, her thoughtfulness, and her genuine concern for his happiness – well, it's truly a beautiful thing.

A woman came in the door of Joe's and greeted Lester, and he her. As she walked by the table she had her head cocked and her eyebrow raised. Her expression read, 'I'm watching you'. Then for some reason she felt the need to say, "Keep your hands on the table, Lester."

The good natured chide pleased Lester. He obediently slammed his big bear paws on the table palms down and made sure both were visible as he laughed at the women who wagged her finger at him.

Mitzi explained, "If I see his hands in his lap I say, 'Lester, what's our rule?'. He's supposed to keep his hands where I can see them." After getting her bra strap snapped, Mitzi's a touch gun shy. No explanation was given for the other woman.

Lester's son, Chester once disclosed, "It all just a bunch of B.S."

Whatever it was, all of the involved parties appeared to have enjoyed the exchanges.

To observe Lester, is to see that much of his life is lived like it's a party - he knows how to maximize the enjoyment of his social time, and business time, more than most. His hearty laughter, his jovial demeanor, his good natured jokes and greetings, that's the side of him that people see most often. But Lester is a man whose emotional pendulum swings equally in both directions. Whether he's saddened by loss or betrayal, or touched by kindness, Lester takes things to heart. Emotion undulates just under the surface. Though words became choked in his throat at those times, when he told of someone who did something nice for him, his gratitude was evident in his eyes.

"There's a lady, I can't forget who was there when I needed her," Lester commented. "She helped me through my emotion to understand things when I most need it."

LESTER ROUGEOT AND NICOLE PAZDAN
JOE'S PLACE PASO ROBLES

Nicole Pazdan, a professional woman, whose elder placement service had helped Lester with arrangements for Barbara's room at Ada's Vineyard, kindly took Lester's well-being to heart, even after he lost Barbara. Nicole's knowledge of the intense love and devotion Lester had for his wife, along with Nicole's understanding of the grieving process, and compassion for a vulnerable man who was no longer a client, but a friend pained beyond measure, drove her to join him for breakfast at Joe's Place on a weekly basis. There she would comfort Lester with her supportive presence.

"I can never thank her enough for her wisdom and knowing what to say and do. My hat is off to her. She is a wonderful person," Lester stated. "God bless you, Nicole Pazdan."

And God bless Joe, Mitzi, Rosie, Debbie, Erica, Char, Diane, Salina, Danielle, Kayla, and Destiny, as well as Joe's kitchen staff. All have helped Lester start his days with smiles and laughter. All have humored this man who, every chance he gets, puts on his poker face and bluffs them into wondering if he's serious or not when he orders something out of the ordinary.

Like at lunch one day.

"I'll have a salad," Lester ordered. As Rosie turned to place his order, Lester continued, "But I don't want no lettuce in there."

LESTER ROUGEOT AND JOE ONTIVEROS

THE FAMILY TREE

DEEP ROOTS

We call upon our forefather's and foremother's stories, our deepest roots, for inspiration so that we might endure hardships or muster the courage to blaze new trails, as they did. We shine light on the people we come from and suddenly life is explainable and the world makes sense. When we relate to a relative, no matter how many years, decades, or centuries ago they lived, we are somehow validated.

The following information is based on intensive genealogical research done by Lester Rougeot's first born child, Regina Rougeot Bonds. As a result of her commitment and loyalty she documented her family's history. Credit is due to Regina for finding ancestors as far back as 1650.

THE ROUGEOT CLAN by Regina Rougeot Bonds

Francis Noel Rougeot was born 1795 in Alsace-Lorraine, France, and Anne Baptiste Raveitt was born 1800 in Alsace-Lorraine, France. Francis and Anne were married about 1824 in France.

Francis died 24, October 1924 in Rome (Ridge Mills), Oneida County, New York. Anne died 11, June 1877 in Rome (Ridge Mills), Oneida, New York. They came to the United States in 1832, settling in Floyd, New York.

They had seven children - John Theodore, Margaret, Cadet T., Eloise B., Catherine, Adel, and Francis.

Cadet Tousse Rougeot was born about 1829 in Alsace-Lorraine, France. Sarah E. Cooley was born about 1830 in Ireland and came to the USA at the age of nine from Cork County, Ireland, and they were married 1 September, 1849 in Rome, New York. Cadet died 6 May, 1877 in Rome, Oneida County, New York of a perforated ulcer of his stomach. Sarah passed away after 1903 in Rome, New York. After Cadet's death, Sarah married Ellery Brown.

Cadet Rougeot was a sawyer, carpenter/building contractor, and was quite well to do at one time until he lost everything and became a farmer. Sarah was a housewife. They had nine children - John, Theodore, Amelia, Eliza, Mary, Thomas, Francis P., Adel, and Noel.

John was born in 1851. He never married and is buried at the Pleasant Valley Cemetery, San Luis Obispo County, California. He was a farmer. Theodore 1 was born in 1852. He married Mary A. Seaton who died at the age of twenty-two on 13 December, 1878. After Mary's death John and Theodore went to Colorado and worked in lumbering for awhile, getting enough money to travel on to the Estrella Plains of California where they farmed/ranched until their deaths.

Eliza married Gerard Jones and passed away at the age of forty-seven due to a "spell in the night". Mary married Daniel Moriarty and passed away at age fifty-nine. Francis P. Rougeot died at the age of 7 by drowning. Lydia Adel was born in 1869 and married Jefferson Brown in 1887.

Thomas Henry Rougeot was born 2 May, 1864 in Glenmore, Oneida County, New York. He married Ida May Shuey, born 29 August 1868, on 14 Oct. 1891 on the Shuey Ranch, Monterey County, California.

Thomas Henry Rougeot's history continued in Chapter One – Granddad's Guidance – page 10.

ROUGEOT FAMILY REUNION – 1937
LESTER ROUGEOT FAR RIGHT BOTTOM ROW

BACK ROW – CLARENCE, ADA, FRANK, FAY, AND RAY
FRONT ROW – IDA MAY AND THOMAS ROUGEOT
1937

IDA MAY AND THOMAS ROUGEOT
SAN LUIS OBISPO – 1937

ROUGEOT FAMILY REUNION
LESTER ROUGEOT BACK ROW FAR RIGHT HELD UP BY
MART TAYLOR

ROUGEOT FAMILY REUNION
LESTER ROUGEOT FAR LEFT BOTTOM ROW

Lester Ralph Rougeot
b: 20 Jul 1925 in Lowes Canyon, Monterey County, California
m: 09 Apr 1946 in Paso Robles, CA
d:

Clarence Theodore Rougeot
b: 02 Nov 1901 in Hog Canyon, Monterey County, CA
m: 05 Nov 1922 in Feeman Home, Hog Canyon, Monterey Co. CA
d: 21 Sep 1964 in Paso Robles, San Luis Obispo, California, USA

Sarah Thelma Freeman
b: 09 Dec 1903 in Globe, Arizona
d: 05 Dec 1998 in Templeton, CA

Thomas Henry Rougeot
b: 02 May 1864 in Glenmore, New York
m: 14 Dec 1891 in Shuey Ranch, Echo Canyon, San Luis Obispo Co. CA
d: 03 May 1948 in San Luis Obispo, California, USA

Ida May Shuey
b: 29 Aug 1868 in Alamo, Contro Costa Co., CA
d: 01 Mar 1951 in San Luis Obispo, California, USA

Rega Dent Freeman
b: 24 Dec 1874 in Indian Spring, Butts, Georgia, USA
m: 26 Sep 1897 in Palo Pinto Co., Texas
d: 12 Apr 1945 in Atascadero, San Luis Obispo, California, USA

Malissa Dovie Nicklas
b: 18 Nov 1878 in Palo Pinto Co., Texas
d: 31 May 1958 in Paso Robles, San Luis Obispo, California, USA

Cadet Tossie Rougeot
b: 1828 in Paris, France
m: 1849
d: 1876 in Rome, New York

Sara Cooley
b: 1830 in Cork County, Ireland
d: 1903

Josephus Martin Shuey
b: 25 Jun 1835 in Bloomfield, Illinois
m: 04 Sep 1856 in Quincy, Ill
d: 11 Jan 1894 in Hog Canyon, San Miguel, CA

Sarah Newland
b: 30 May 1839
d: 09 Oct 1929 in San Luis Obispo, California, USA

Thomas Francis Hearne Freeman
b: 25 Jul 1850 in Indian Spring,....
m: 17 Mar 1874 in Monroe Co.,....
d: 17 Dec 1921 in Gaines,....

Mary Susan Brown
b: Monroe Co., Georgia
d: 16 Apr 1936 in Gaines, Michigan

William David Nicklas
b: 24 Mar 1848 in Alabama, USA
m: 28 Sep 1869 in Farmville, Louisiana
d: 29 Oct 1863 in Indianapolis, Indiana

Epsy Melton
b: 15 Jun 1853 in Alabama, USA
d: 05 Jan 1921 in McAdams Cemetery, Pickwick, Texas

THE FREEMAN CLAN by Regina Rougeot Bonds

John F. Freeman was born about 1650 in England and married about 1679 in Norfolk, Virginia to Hannah Hurdle. They had one son – William, who married Mary Cording. They had six children - William Thomas, Aaron, John, Richard, and Thomas P.

Thomas P. married Sarah Low Wingate in Norfork, Virginia. They had a son - Josiah.

Thomas P. Freeman brought the family to Monroe County, Georgia. He served in the War of 1812 and was otherwise prominently identified with his state until his death. He was of Scot Irish descent. He served as a volunteer - Captain First Regiment North Carolina Detached Militia of Gates County.

Josiah Freeman was born in North Carolina and was an overseer on a plantation. He married Sarah W. Hearn, who was born in Putnam County, Georgia. After his marriage Josiah became a cotton planter and had three thousand acres on his plantation when the Civil War broke out. The war made such inroads upon his fortune and property, destroying all that he had, that he never recovered his financial position, dying at the age of seventy-one years of age. Josiah and Sarah had ten children - Thomas Francis, Josia, William, James, John, Pirponed, Seplinus, Jesse, Oskes, and Sallie.

Thomas Francis Freeman was born in Indian Springs, Butts County, Georgia on July 25, 1850 to Josiah and Sarah W. Hearn Freeman. He attended subscription school until the war broke out, when there were no advantages at all for getting an education. After the war, he studied for a time and continued at home assisting his father until he was twenty-four when he married Miss Susan Brown who was born in Monroe County, Georgia. The ancestors of the Brown family came from England and were members of the Oglethorpe colony in Georgia.

Thomas Francis Freeman's history continued in Chapter One - Granddad's Guidance page 6.

ONA, DOVIE, MARGARET, THELMA – INDIAN VALLEY

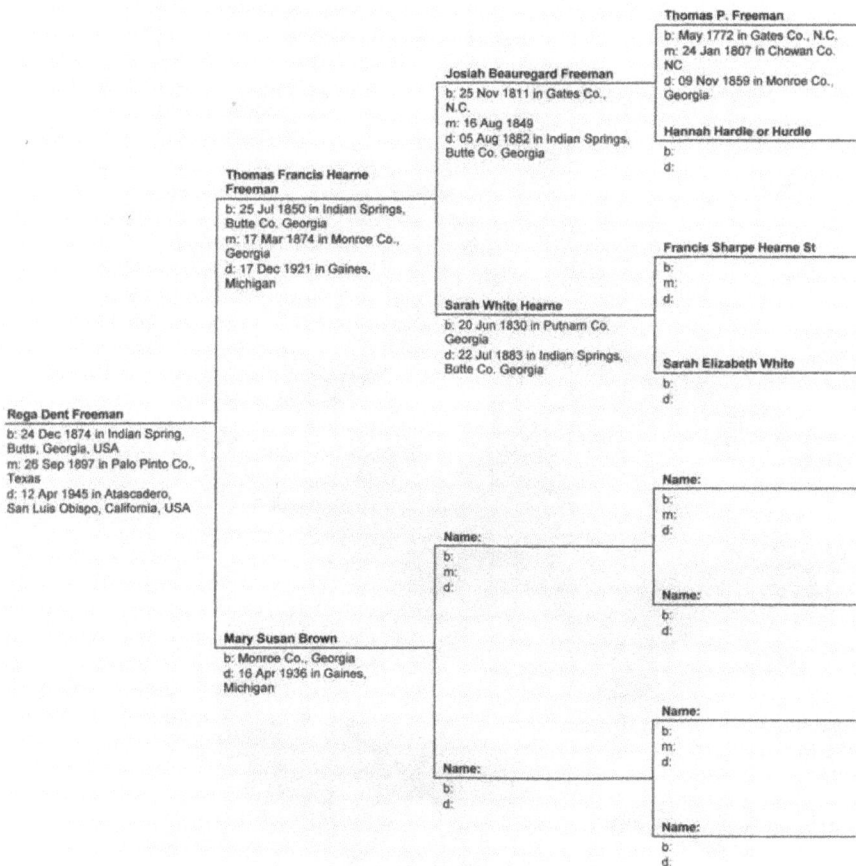

Rega Dent Freeman
b: 24 Dec 1874 in Indian Spring, Butts, Georgia, USA
m: 26 Sep 1897 in Palo Pinto Co., Texas
d: 12 Apr 1945 in Atascadero, San Luis Obispo, California, USA

Thomas Francis Hearne Freeman
b: 25 Jul 1850 in Indian Springs, Butte Co. Georgia
m: 17 Mar 1874 in Monroe Co., Georgia
d: 17 Dec 1921 in Gaines, Michigan

Mary Susan Brown
b: Monroe Co., Georgia
d: 16 Apr 1936 in Gaines, Michigan

Josiah Beauregard Freeman
b: 25 Nov 1811 in Gates Co., N.C.
m: 16 Aug 1849
d: 05 Aug 1882 in Indian Springs, Butte Co. Georgia

Sarah White Hearne
b: 20 Jun 1830 in Putnam Co. Georgia
d: 22 Jul 1883 in Indian Springs, Butte Co. Georgia

Name:
b:
m:
d:

Name:
b:
d:

Thomas P. Freeman
b: May 1772 in Gates Co., N.C.
m: 24 Jan 1807 in Chowan Co. NC
d: 09 Nov 1859 in Monroe Co., Georgia

Hannah Hardle or Hurdle
b:
d:

Francis Sharpe Hearne St
b:
m:
d:

Sarah Elizabeth White
b:
d:

Name:
b:
m:
d:

Name:
b:
d:

Name:
b:
m:
d:

Name:
b:
d:

REGA DENT FREEMAN
LESTER ROUGEOT'S MATERNAL GRANDFATHER
More on Rega Dent Freeman in Chapter One – Granddad's Guidance

REGA DENT FREEMAN

MALISSA DOVIE NICKLAS FREEMAN

Malissa Dovie Nicklas
b: 18 Nov 1878 in Palo Pinto Co., Texas
m: 26 Sep 1897 in Palo Pinto Co., Texas
d: 31 May 1958 in Paso Robles, San Luis Obispo, California, USA

William David Nicklas
b: 24 Mar 1848 in Alabama
m: 28 Sep 1869 in Farmersville, LA
d: 30 Jun 1935 in Texas

Wilson David Nicklas
b: 1824 in Jefferson Co. Alabama
m: 02 Jan 1842 in Shelby Co., Alabama
d: 29 Oct 1863 in Indianapolis, Indiana

Joseph "Joel" Nicklas
b: 1800 in Tennessee
m: 23 Mar 1823 in Jefferson Co. Alabama
d: 1855

Mary Ann"Polly" Loveless (lovelace)
b: 26 Jun 1800
d: Aug 1876

Martha Redden
b: 1826 in Shelby Co., Alabama
d: 1905 in Lillie Union, Louisiana

David Redden (Rarden)
b: 1807 in Ohio City, Clermont, Ohio, USA
m:
d: 1891 in Melroy Rush, Indiana

Rachel Lindsey
b: 1810 in Tennessee
d: 1880 in Shelby Co., Alabama

Epsy Melton
b: 15 Jun 1853 in Alabama
d: 05 Jan 1921 in McAdams Cemetry, Pickwick, Texas

Perry Melton
b: Sep 1825 in Twiggs Co., GA
m: 18 Feb 1847 in Bibb Co. Alabama
d: 19 Jun 1885 in Spearville, LA

John Melton
b: 1803 in Kershaw, South Carolina, USA
m:
d:

Name:
b:
d:

Olive Albina Muse
b: 08 Aug 1831 in Alabama
d: 09 Sep 1863 in Spearville, LA

Drury Jackson Muse
b: 15 Nov 1806 in Wilkes Co. Georgia
m: 23 Dec 1827 in Bibb Co. Alabama
d: 1888 in Perry Co. Alabama, Mt. Olive Cem.

Elizabeth M. Hay
b: 16 Oct 1806 in Wilkes Co. Georgia
d: 29 Apr 1885 in Perry Co. Alabama, Mt. Olive Cem.

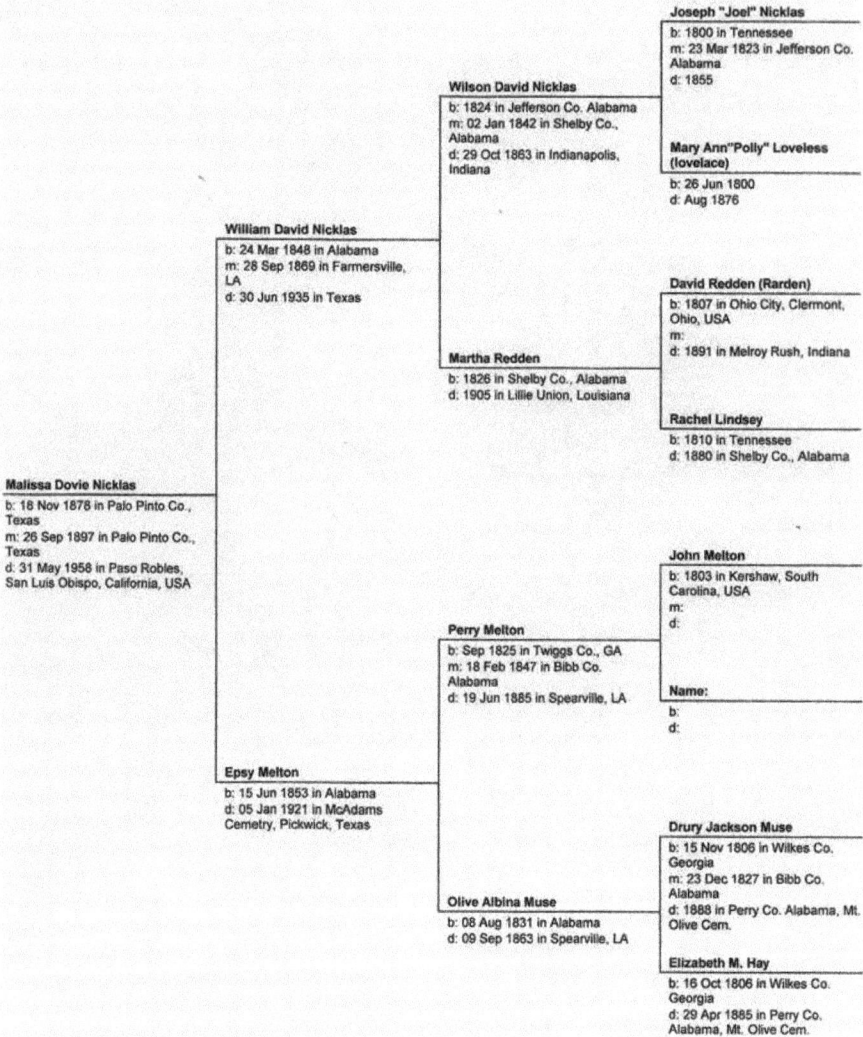

MALISSA DOVIE NICKLAS MARRIED REGA DENT FREEMAN
DOVIE IS LESTER ROUGEOT'S MATERNAL GRANDMOTHER

THE NICKLAS FAMILY

BACK ROW – DOVIE NICKLAS FREEMAN,
CHARLES NICKLAS, BEATIE NICKLAS BYLES, WILLIS NICKLAS,
CLEMMIE NICKLAS WESTIN

MIDDLE ROW – PERRY NICLAS, HENRY NICKLAS,
WILLIAM DAVID NICKLAS, EPSY MELTON NICKLAS,
ELURIE NICKLAS REEVES

FRONT ROW – JEWEL NICKLAS, WINNIE NICKLAS PARCELY

EPSY MELTON NICKLAS
DOVIE NICKLAS FREEMAN'S MOTHER,
LESTER ROUGEOT'S GREAT GRANDMOTHER

WILLIAM DAVID NICKLAS
DOVIE NICKLAS FREEMAN'S FATHER
LESTER ROUGEOT'S GREAT GRANDFATHER

William Pope Muse
b: 1725
m:
d: 1819

George Muse
b: 1780 in Wilkes Co. Georgia
m: 11 Jan 1799 in Wilkes Co. Georgia
d: 1809 in Wilkes Co. Georgia

Mary Pope
b:
d:

Drury Jackson Muse
b: 15 Nov 1806 in Wilkes Co. Georgia
m: 23 Dec 1827 in Bibb Co. Alabama
d: 1888 in Perry Co. Alabama, Mt. Olive Cem.

Drury Wyche Jackson
b: 1751
m:
d: 1794

Elizabeth (Jackson) Sutton
b: 1784 in Wilkes Co. Georgia
d: 1845 in Clarke, Georgia, USA

Nancy Ann Mayfield
b: 1748
d: 1837

Olive Albina Muse
b: 08 Aug 1831 in Alabama
m: 18 Feb 1847 in Bibb Co. Alabama
d: 09 Sep 1863 in Spearville, LA

Hardy Hays
b: 1732
m:
d: 1784

David Hay
b: 1778 in Barnwell, SC
m: 15 Mar 1800 in Wilkes Co. Georgia
d: 02 Feb 1855 in Perry Co. Alabama,

Elizabeth Goodwin
b: 1734
d: 1800

Elizabeth M. Hay
b: 16 Oct 1806 in Wilkes Co. Georgia
d: 29 Apr 1885 in Perry Co. Alabama, Mt. Olive Cem.

Willis Pope
b: 1754 in Halifax, N.C.
m:
d: 1795 in Welles, GA

Winnifred (Winnie) Pope
b: 1784 in Wilkes Co. Georgia
d: 18 Apr 1851 in Perry Co. Alabama,

Mary Glover
b: 1760 in Halifax, N.C.
d: 1801

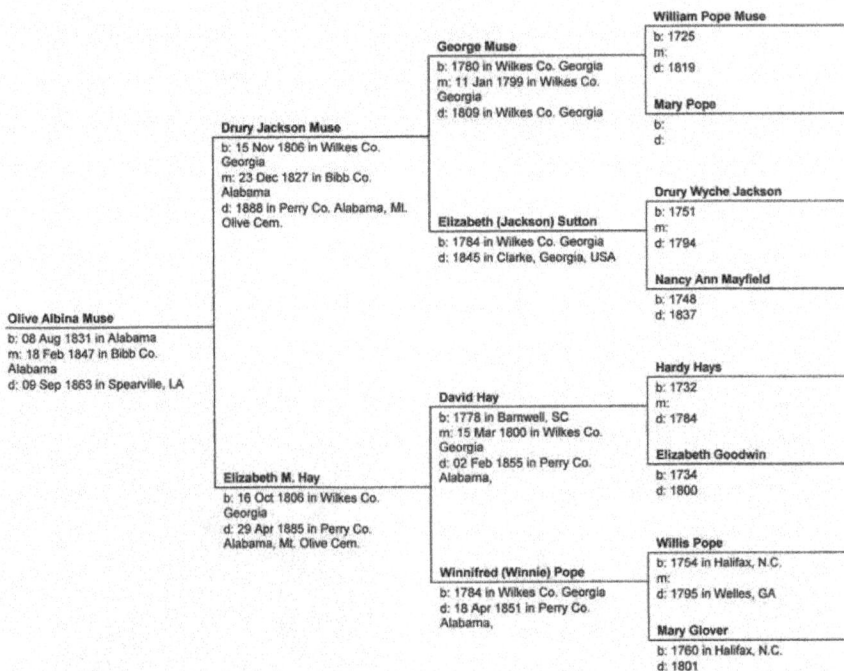

OLIVE MUSE IS EPSY MELTON NICKLAS MOTHER, DOVIE NICKLAS FREEMAN'S GRANDMOTHER

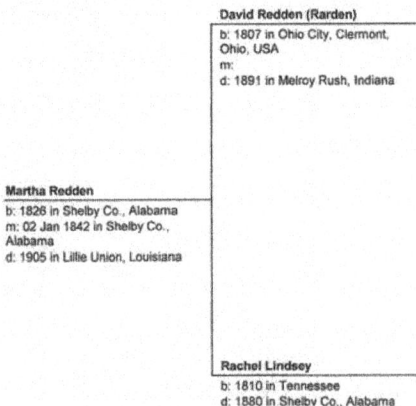

David Redden (Rarden)
b: 1807 in Ohio City, Clermont, Ohio, USA
m:
d: 1891 in Melroy Rush, Indiana

Martha Redden
b: 1826 in Shelby Co., Alabama
m: 02 Jan 1842 in Shelby Co., Alabama
d: 1905 in Lillie Union, Louisiana

Rachel Lindsey
b: 1810 in Tennessee
d: 1880 in Shelby Co., Alabama

MARTHA REEDEN MOTHER TO WILLIAM DAVID NICKLAS II, LESTER ROUGEOT'S GREAT GREAT GRANDMOTHER

THE SHUEY CLAN by Regina Rougeot Bonds

Family patriarch, Daniel Schuy, arrived in Philadelphia on Sept. 18, 1732, aboard the Johnson from Rotterdam (in the Netherlands - one of the largest ports of the world). He was born about April 6, 1703 in Oggersheim, in the Palatinate, and lived there and later in Darmstadt. His French Huguenot (French Protestant) parents and grandparents had immigrated to present-day Germany circa 1695 to escape brutal Catholic persecution.

The Shueys took an active role in the American Revolution, seeing action on both sides of the Civil War. They helped settle the frontier west. Today, there is a Shuey Run, Shuey Lake in Pennsylvania, Shueyville in Iowa, Shuey Avenue in Walnut Creek, California, Mount Shuey and Shuey Pass in Jasper Nation Park, Connecticut, and a Shuey School in California.

Daniel Schuy married Maria Margaretha Schilling who was born Oct. 16, 1775 in Darmstadt, Pfalz, DEU (Germany). When he arrived in the United States of America he was unable to write his name and between the language barrier and the clerk's bungled attempt the Schuy name was spelled eight or more different ways here in the USA. Going from Juy or Jouy to Schwe and Schuhy and Shewey then in the late 1700's it seemed to settle on Schuy and finally it emerged to Shuey. Nine children were born to this union - Ludwick Heinrich, Anna Margaretta, Johannes, Martin, Peter, Margaret, Barbara, Daniel and Catharine.

Ludwick Heinrich (Lewis Henry) Schuy was born Oct. 12, 1726 in Darmstadt, Pfaiz, DEU (Germany). He married Elizabeth. In 1771, Bethel Township, he is listed as having four hundred acres, five horses and six cows. They had five children - John Henry, John Martin, Christian, Catherin, John Adam.

John Martin Shuey was born June 20, 1750 in Bethel Township, Lancaster County, PB and married Margaret Elizabeth Conrad, born 1741-1765, in 1779 in Pennsylvania. Their children were - John Big John, Catherine, Christina, General Martin, Barbara, Margaret, Henry, Mary, Eve, and Adam.

John served in the 3rd Company Battalion, Lancaster County Militia in 1780 American Revolution. In 1805 he moved his family to

Germantown, Ohio area.

General Martin Shuey was born September 25, 1785, in Bethel, Dauphin County., Pennsylvania and Mary Margaret Shupert, born Feb. 22, 1788 in Philadelphia, Pennsylvania, and married in 1808 in Ohio Their children were - John, Henry, Olivia, Samuel David, Robert, Jacob, and Melvia.

Martin was a Brigadier General in the War of 1812.

Henry Shuey was born November 9, 1812, in Montgomery County, Ohio and Sarah Stowe, born about 1809 in Chester, Massachusetts and married in 1834. They had five children - Lucetta Ann, Josephus Martin, Margaret Lucretia, William Henry, and Edward Jacob.

Josephus Martin Shuey was born June 25, 1835 in Illinois and married Sarah Newland who was born about 1839. They were married September 4, 1856 in Adams, Illinois. They had three children - Lucella J., Emma C., and Ida May.

Lucella married James E. Gorham, Emma married T.A. Rude, and Ida May married Thomas Henry Rougeot. Ida May Shuey was born August 29, 1868 at the Shuey Home in Estrella, San Luis Obispo County, California.

IDA MAY SHUEY

236

SARAH NEWLAND
IDA MAY SHUEY ROUGEOT'S MOTHER
LESTER ROUGEOT'S GREAT GRANDMOTHER

Ida May Shuey's history continued in Chapter One – Granddad's Guidance – page 10.

Brig. Gen. Martin Shuey
b: 28 Sep 1785 in Dauphine, Lebanon Co. PA
m: 30 Jun 1808
d: 12 Feb 1876 in Fruitvale, Oakland, CA

Henry Shuey
b: 09 Nov 1812 in Montgomery Co., Ohio
m: 31 Aug 1834
d: 18 Oct 1884 in Walnut Creek, Contra Costa, California, USA

Mary Margaret Shupert
b: 22 Feb 1788 in Montgomery Co. Ohio
d: 29 Nov 1878 in Fruitvale, Oakland, CA

Josephus Martin Shuey
b: 25 Jun 1835 in Bloomfield, Illinois
m: 04 Sep 1856 in Quincy, Ill
d: 11 Jan 1894 in Hog Canyon, San Miguel, CA

Name:
b:
m:
d:

Sarah Stowe
b: Jul 1806 in Adams Co. Ill
d: 31 Aug 1868 in Walnut Creek, Contra Costa, California, USA

Name:
b:
d:

Ida May Shuey
b: 29 Aug 1868 in Alamo, Contra Costa Co., CA
m: 14 Dec 1891 in Shuey Ranch, Echo Canyon, San Luis Obispo Co. CA
d: 01 Mar 1951 in San Luis Obispo, California, USA

Name:
b:
m:
d:

Name:
b:
d:

Name:
b:
m:
d:

Sarah Newland
b: 30 May 1839
d: 09 Oct 1929 in San Luis Obispo, California, USA

Name:
b:
d:

Name:
b:
m:
d:

Name:
b:
d:

Name:
b:
m:
d:

Name:
b:
d:

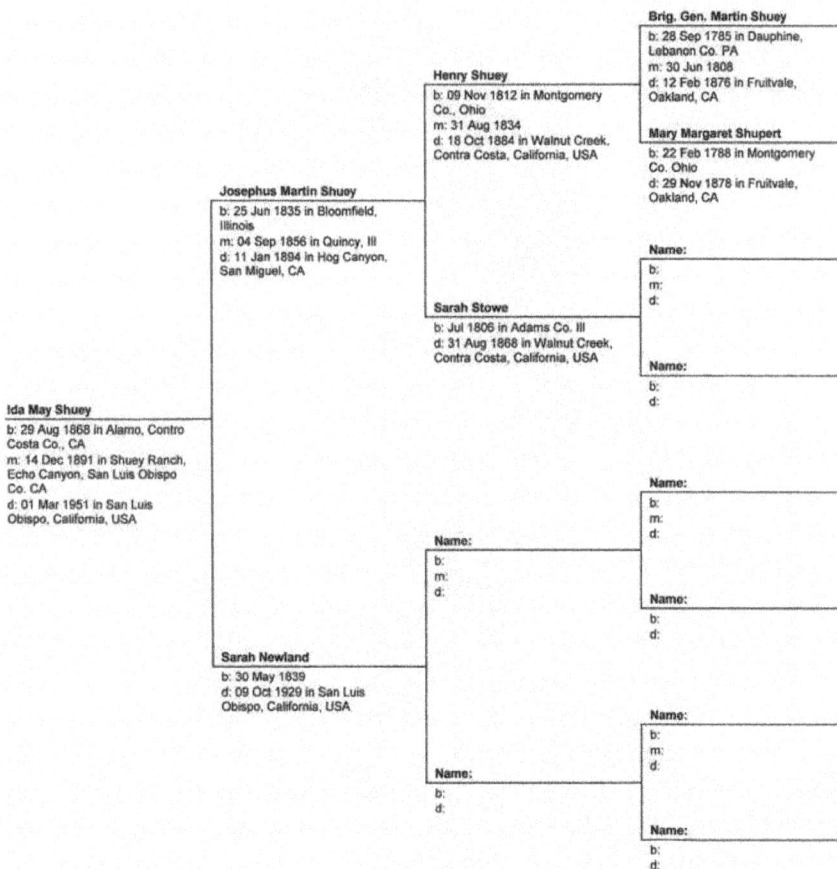

IDA MAY SHUEY ROUGEOT
LESTER ROUGEOT'S PATERNAL GRANDMOTHER

NEW FOLIAGE

Generations of the future - the promise of new foliage, signs of life on our family trees.

REGINA, CHESTER, MARGIE, BARBARA, AND LESTER
THE ROUGEOTS AT EL PASO DE ROBLES GRANGE #555
1996

THE BONDS FAMILY

BACK ROW – BOBBY, DONNIE, MIKE
MIDDLE ROW – JACOB, KELLEY, HAILEY, SAMANATHA, TRISTAN
BOTTOM ROW – MICAH, REGINA, JORDAN

FIVE GENERATIONS
REGINA ROUGEOT BONDS, SAMANTHA BONDS, LESTER
ROUGEOT, THELMA ROUGEOT, MIKE BONDS

BARBARA AND LESTER ROUGEOT WITH THEIR
GREAT GRANDCHILDREN JACOB, HAILEY, AND
SAMANTHA BONDS

KELLEY BONDS WITH GRANDSON TRISTAN XAVIER BONDS
SON OF ROBERT BONDS AND EMILY MEMMIT

MIKE, DONNIE, AND BOBBY BONDS

MICHAEL KELLEY BONDS

LESTER ROUGEOT WITH GREAT GRANDDAUGHTER
SAMANTHA BONDS

SAMANTHA MARIE BONDS - 2011
FLOYD COUNTY VIRGINIA
CROSS BOW HUNTER
DAUGHTER OF MICHAEL BONDS AND JENNIFER GAYLE BUTLER

ALYSSA BARNETT AND ROBERT DALE BONDS

JORDAN ELIZABETH AND MICAH NICHOLAS BONDS
DEER HUNTERS
DAUGHTER AND SON OF ROBERT BONDS AND EMILY JESSICA MEMMIT

HAILEY MORGAN BONDS
TROUT FISHERMAN
DAUGHTER OF DONALD BONDS AND CYNTHIA RAE KIRKNER

VICTOR LEROUX AND MARGIE ROUGEOT LEROUX,
BARBARA AND LESTER ROUGEOT,
REGINA ROUGEOT BONDS AND KELLEY BONDS

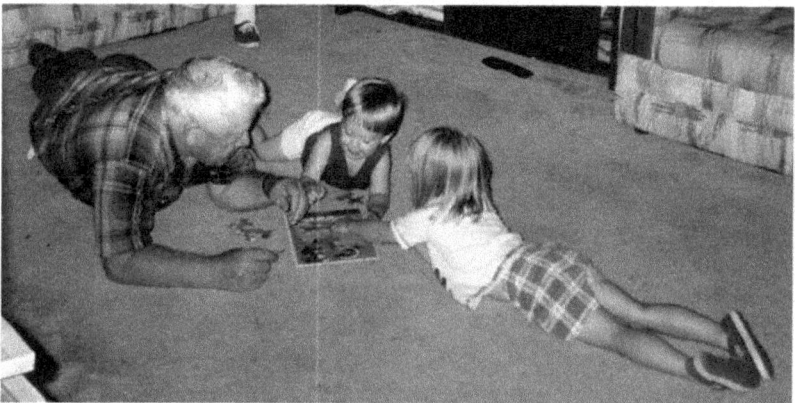

LESTER ROUGEOT WITH GREAT GRANDCHILDREN
JACOB DONALD BONDS AND HAILEY MORGAN BONDS
CHILDREN OF DONALD LESTER BONDS AND CYNTHIA RAE KIRKNER

DONNIE BONDS AND KIM DELP 2012

CHESTER AND LESTER ROUGEOT
LOWES CANYON FEBRUARY 2012

LOUISE MARIE HARTZELL ROUGEOT AND CHESTER ROUGEOT

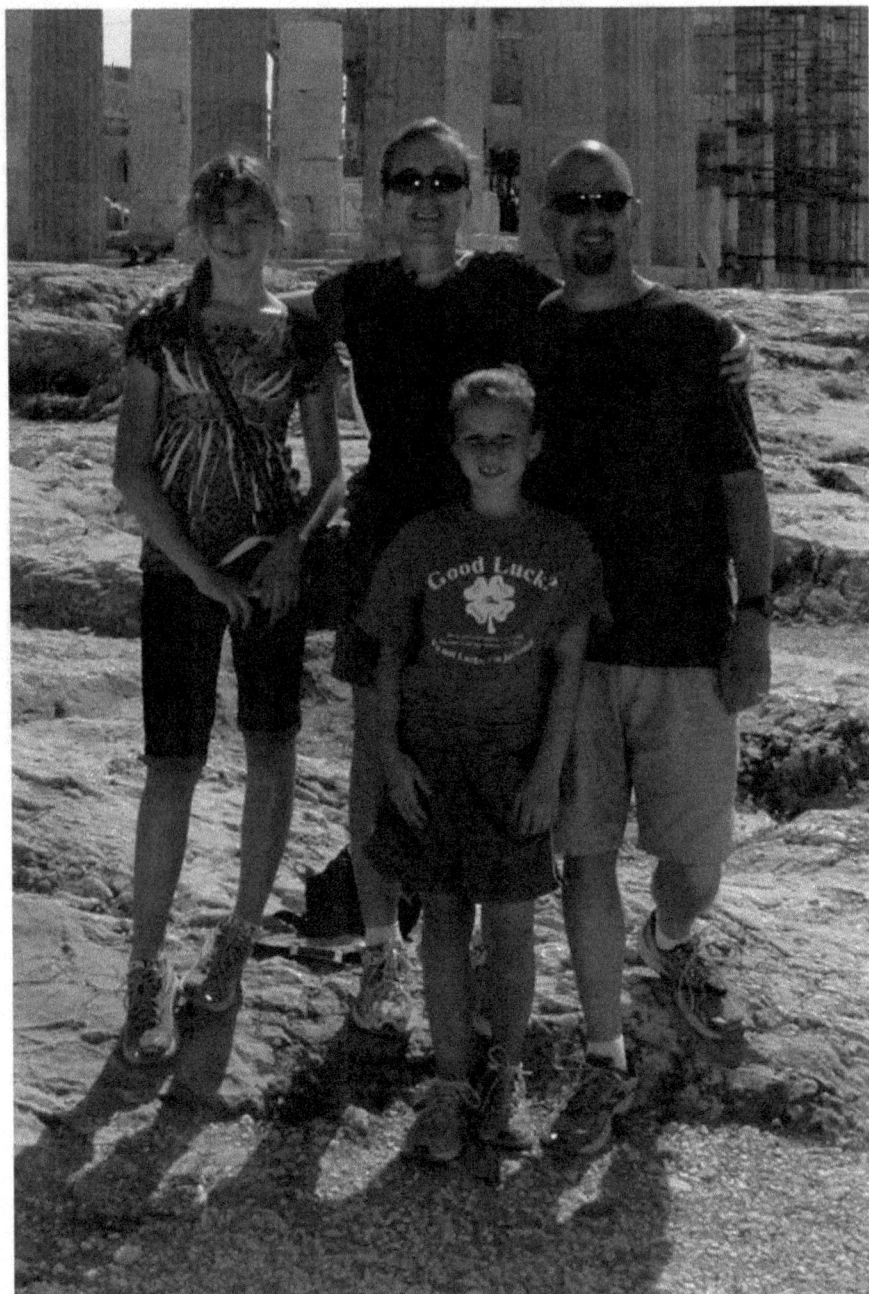

THE WALSH FAMILY
SYDNEY, MARY REGINA ROUGEOT WALSH, JAMES,
AND SARA IN FRONT
MARY IS THE DAUGHTER OF CHESTER AND LOUISE ROUGEOT

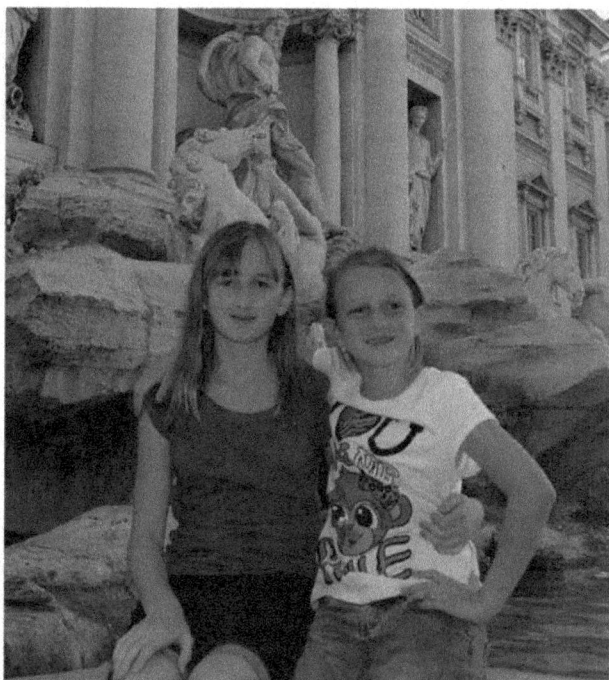

SYDNEY AND SARA WALSH
GREAT GRANDDAUGHTERS OF LESTER ROUGEOT

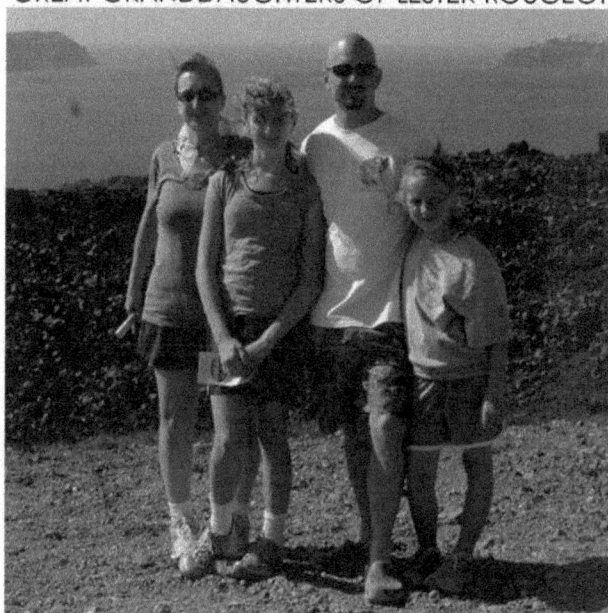

THE WALSH FAMILY
MARY, SYDNEY, JAMES, AND SARA

MARGIE ROUGEOT LEROUX AND VICTOR LEROUX

VICTOR LEROUX AND MARGIE ROUGEOT LEROUX
WEDDING
KARATE BROTHERS AND SISTERS - JIM TAYLOR BEHIND WITH SHOTGUN

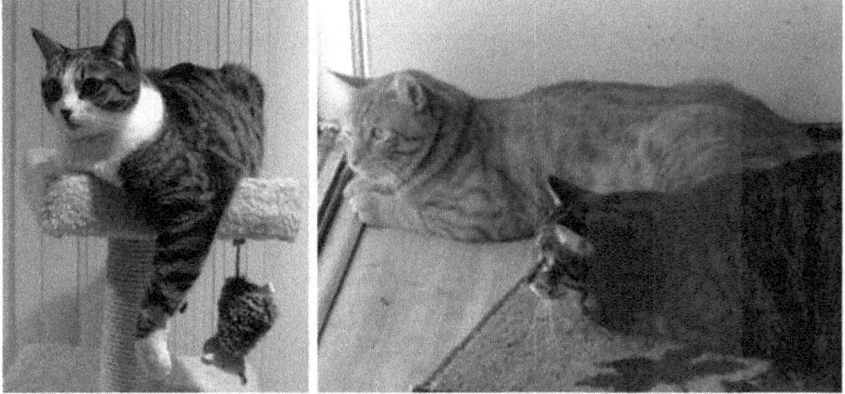

MARGIE ROUGEOT LEROUX'S FELINE "CHILDREN"
SHEELA MONSTER, TAZ BO, AND MAXWELL

RAYMOND AND ALICE MILLER AND FAMILY
RAYMOND, ALICE, HARRY, JUDY, AND ROGER MILLER
PARKFIELD - APRIL 24, 1994
JUDY MILLER IS LESTER'S NIECE ALSO KNOWN AS HIS "THIRD DAUGHTER"

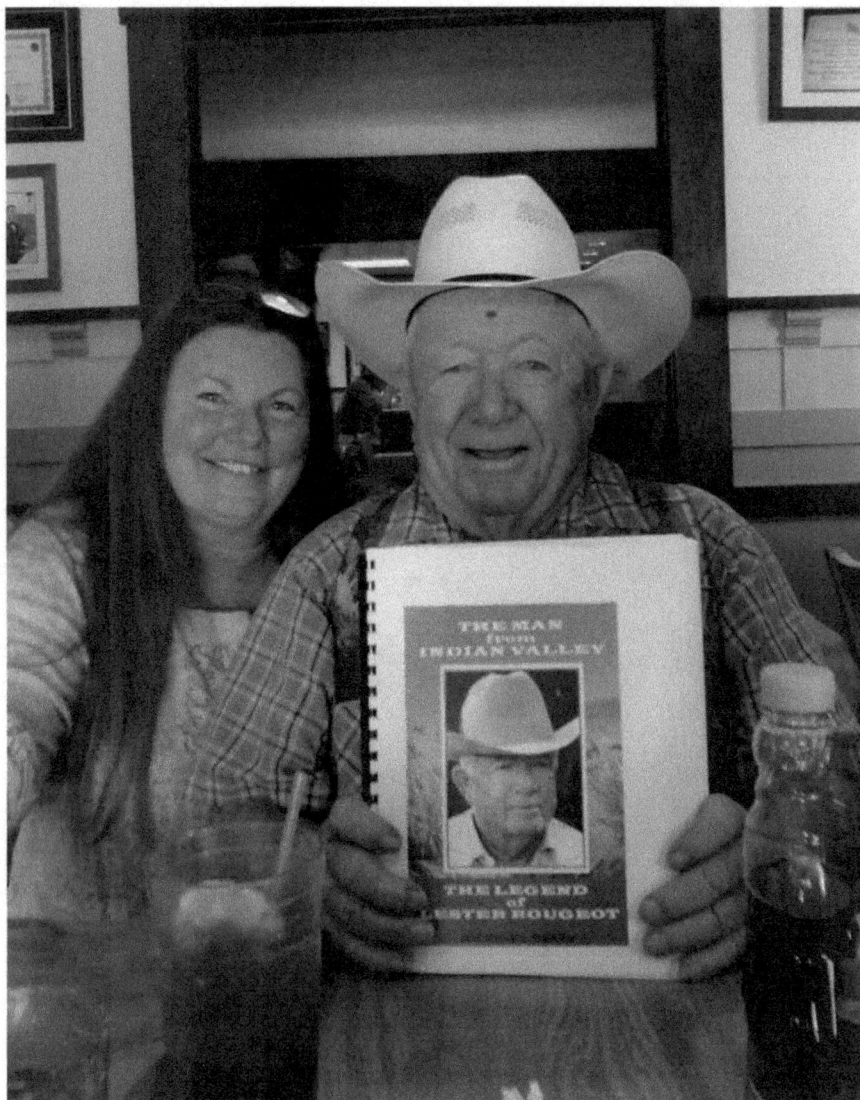

MICHELE OKSEN AND LESTER ROUGEOT
JOE'S PLACE, PASO ROBLES - JULY 2012

ABOUT THE AUTHOR

Michele Oksen is a fourth generation Californian. She lives in the
Santa Lucia Mountains east of Cambria. There she writes a column
called *Mountain Musings,* for The Cambrian newspaper, as well as a
column called *Coastland Contemplations,* for an online publication,
SloCoastJournal.com
Michele has written two fictional novels - *The Secrets of Misty Creek
and Buckle Bunny Blues.* Both are in the process of edits and rewrites
and are expected to be published in 2013.